The Films of
ALFRED
HITCHCOCK

The Films of
ALFRED HITCHCOCK

PATRICK HUMPHRIES

Crescent Books
New York/Avenel, New Jersey

Page 1: *Echoing the last scene from his last film,* Family Plot *(1976), the inimitable Alfred Hitchcock.*
Pages 2-3: *Barbara Harris and Bruce Dern in the chase scene from* Family Plot.
Page 4: *Cary Grant in North by Northwest (1959).*

This 1994 edition published by Crescent Books, distributed by Outlet Book Company, Inc., a Random House Company, 40 Engelhard Avenue Avenel, New Jersey 07001

Produced by
Brompton Books Corporation
15 Sherwood Place
Greenwich, CT 06830

ISBN 0-517-10292-7

Printed and bound in China

To Susan Parr, with much love and many thanks for all that follows; her erudite editing and auterism helped shape the rumour, myth, madness and love that lie on the road to Manderley . . .

AUTHOR'S ACKNOWLEDGMENTS

Inordinate thanks to Hazel Griffith at CIC Home Video for her help in setting wheels in motion.
Kind thanks to the following, whose generous loan of videos made the task of writing actually pleasant for once: Delora Spierin, the vanishing lady from Rank; Judy Kneale, aka Kathleen Turner, from Warner Home Video; Margaret Beveridge from Guild Home Video; Sue Nicola for 'Blackmail,' at Thorn-EMI Screen Entertainment and Amanda Slayton at Mathieu Thomas.
To Sean Bell-Briggs, for playing a bumnote there . . . , Mr & Mrs Andrew Whitfield (The Jeweller & Niki) for inspiration and encouragement; Mark Seaman, Dick Wallis and Sally-Anne Jones, with fond memories of the NFT in the 1970s; Lawrence Morphet and Michael Green and the old East Dulwich Odeon and Norah & Geoff, with thanks for curtains, cleaning and carpentry.

January 1986

CONTENTS

INTRODUCTION

'If once a man indulges himself in murder, very soon he comes to think little of robbery, and from robbery he comes next to drinking and Sabbath-breaking, and from that to incivility and procrastination!'

Thomas de Quincey *On Murder.*

More, perhaps, than any medium, film creates its own world. For two hours an audience sits in a darkened auditorium with no distractions save what the filmmaker wishes displayed on the screen ahead. The audience knows what to expect when they enter that world: the films of Steven Spielberg entrance and mesmerize, in past or future; Woody Allen shares his neuroses for the benefit of others. But as one of a handful of directors whose name is known to the film-going public at large, the films of Alfred Hitchcock create a special world of their own. Nothing is ever quite what it seems in a Hitchcock film – amiable pillars of society are revealed to be manipulative criminals, seemingly honest, upright citizens are shown to be deceitful villains, an innocent man finds himself at the center of a web of doubt and intrigue. The rug is constantly tugged from beneath the audience's feet. Hitchcock himself recognized his reputation: 'If I made Cinderella, the audience would be looking for the body in the coach!'

In a career spanning half a century Hitchcock made over 50 films, and carved himself a niche in cinema history. While audiences kidded themselves they knew what to expect from a Hitchcock film, they were deluding themselves: they knew they would not get a musical – although, with typical aplomb, Hitchcock even turned his hand to that in *Waltzes From Vienna*; they knew it would not be a comedy – although Hitchcock insisted that he saw *Psycho* as a comedy! No, they went along to be scared, thrilled; if there was a lull, it was only to trick the audience into a false sense of security. In *Psycho*, his most successful film, the heroine is killed a mere third of the way into the film, and with the star dead that sense of security lapses even further.

Left: *Hitchcock seen during the filming of* Family Plot *(1976).*

Perhaps *Rear Window* (1954) stands as the finest example of Alfred Hitchcock's craft. Technically dazzling, with an edge-of-seat narrative and exemplary performances, it shows the spellbinding authority of a director at the peak of his form. While his other films may occupy a place in the viewer's affection, *Rear Window* particularly reveals just *why* Hitchcock was such a master. When Alfred Hitchcock died in 1980, cinema was robbed of the last of the great directors whose careers began in silent films, thereby embracing the very history of cinema itself.

Hitchcock was an unpredictable director but his work can be neatly divided into two eras – his films (both silent and sound) in Great Britain between the wars, and the American films which brought his name to the world from the 1940s onward. Hitchcock's films reflect his own anxieties and neuroses and gave him the opportunity to stop being a shy, obese misogynist and become a film director, a god with power over women and the ability to manipulate narrative, time and character to his own ends. His reputation as a cold, calculating manipulator of emotions is at odds with an incident Joseph Stefano, the writer of *Psycho*, told of dropping Hitchcock outside a hotel where he was unable to find a cab to take him home. The image Stefano was left with was of Alfred Hitchcock terrified and alone, like a character from one of his own films, unable to direct the next scene.

Alfred Hitchcock was a complex individual. Essentially a private man, there is much of the man in his films, which stand as his living testament. Despite biographies which delineate the obsessive, sadistic side of his nature, Hitchcock was one of the few outright geniuses cinema has given us. His 50-odd films testify to that; many are as fresh, chilling and invigorating today as they were when first released. That is the legacy of Alfred Hitchcock.

THE SILENT YEARS

Alfred Joseph Hitchcock was born in the east London area of Leytonstone on 13 August 1899, the youngest son of a mildly prosperous fruiterer and greengrocer. His brother William was nine years older, and his sister Nellie was almost seven years older. Hitchcock was very much a child of the Victorian era and his birth virtually coincides with that of the cinema itself. The year that Hitchcock was born, Britain entered the Second Boer War on a wave of jingoism and the Kaiser visited his aunt, Queen Victoria, at Sandringham.

It is perhaps fanciful to establish Hitchcock as a child of the Victorian era; he was, after all, only 4 months old when the 19th century became the 20th, and a mere 17 months when Edward VII succeeded Queen Victoria. But the long summer of Edwardian England was a different world, retaining a vestige of the 19th century which ended only with the bloody outbreak of World War I in 1914. The heyday of the Edwardian summer saw the *Titanic* briefly sail the high seas, the Wright Brothers take to the air in 1903 and narrative cinema begin with Edwin S Porter's 12-minute *Great Train Robbery* (1903). Interestingly, this film ended with a character turning his pistol on the audience and firing at them, a device Hitchcock used in *Spellbound* over 40 years later.

Hitchcock grew up a solitary child. Despite having an older brother and sister, the age difference was such that he frequently had to rely on his own company. The young Alfred enjoyed the detective fiction of John Buchan, Conan Doyle and G K Chesterton, while frowning on the 'lowbrow' Sexton Blake. His affection for his mother has been well recorded and his relations with his father were cordial, if remote. However, his relationship with his father has taken on a sinister aspect owing to Hitchcock's famous story of an incident from his childhood. When he was five years old, after some minor misdemeanor, Hitchcock's father sent him round to the local police station with a note, which the boy in all innocence handed to the station sergeant. He was promptly locked up in a cell for 10 minutes, with the warning, 'This is what we do to naughty boys!' Hitchcock loved telling this tale himself in later years and many interpreters of his work have seen this as a seminal incident from his childhood. It has been overplayed in later years, for Hitchcock certainly never bore his father any permanent ill-feeling and the event had no lasting psychological effect, save for giving Hitchcock a lifelong mistrust of the police and uniformed authority in general. Certainly the innocent wrongly imprisoned materializes in many Hitchcock films, most notably in the uncharacteristic documentary *The Wrong Man* (1957). Hitchcock himself said in later years: 'The theme of the innocent being accused, I feel, provides the audience with a greater sense of danger. It's easier for them to identify with him than a guilty man on the run.'

The Hitchcocks were an Irish Catholic family, and the young Alfred was dutifully dispatched to local Jesuit schools before spending five years at St Ignatius College in north London. He was an average student, and retained his insularity, recalling that he never had a playmate and used to invent all his own games. The old Jesuit maxim 'Give me the child and I'll give you the man' was not fulfilled in Hitchcock's case. Although he was never irreligious in his films, clergymen represented authority, and Hitchcock saw them as figures of amusement and poked fun at the rituals surround-

ing the clergy right up to his last film. In *Family Plot* (1976), made when he was nearly 80, Hitchcock had a bishop kidnapped during a service. Later in life though, Hitchcock pointed out through a car window to his companion 'The most frightening sight I have ever seen' – actually nothing more sinister than a priest talking to a small boy. Apparently Hitchcock leant out of the car and shouted 'Run, little boy, run for your life!'

Hitchcock certainly did not excel at school and left at 16 to study engineering. With the specter of World War I hovering over him and his generation (Hitchcock failed his army medical in 1917) and the terrible influenza epidemic which swept Britain immediately after the Armistice, the future did not look rosy. His first real job was with the Henley Telegraph Company, which specialized in making electric cables. He took evening classes in art and drawing at the University of London.

The solitary child was already shaping into the portly, insular young man. By his late teens, Hitchcock was fascinated by the cinema, a usually solitary occupation, and proudly read all the technical film magazines he could obtain. However, he shied away from the more popular fan magazines, although he had fond memories of such stars as Charlie Chaplin, Buster Keaton, Mary Pickford and Douglas Fairbanks.

During Hitchcock's adolescence cinema grew from being a novelty squeezed in between turns at variety shows to an art form. Basil Wright recognized that the importance of the cinema was that it 'restored to the great mass of humanity the magic and myths from which it had for so long been cut off.' The massive immigrant populations of England and America sought sanctuary in the early cinemas, seizing the opportunity to escape into the fantasy world this essentially visual medium offered. Literacy played no part, and in the exuberant fantasies of Georges Méliès and the like, largely working-class audiences escaped their stifling poverty. Cinema offered a cheap but exotic escape from the poverty of their workaday existence, allowing them to enter worlds they could previously only imagine.

In 1914 fellow-cockney Charles Chaplin donned his immortal tramp costume for the first time and, while Europe tore itself apart in World War I, American cinema achieved its stranglehold on the world market. Stars were born and by the 1920s Valentino, Pickford, Fairbanks, Chaplin and others were truly household names. In Russia Sergei Eisenstein's masterpieces such as *Strike* (1925) and *Battleship Potemkin* (1925) were forged in the white heat of revolution, and Lenin proclaimed the cinema the most important art form. Truly, the cinema grew up with the 20th century. Not until the 1980s were audiences able to appreciate again the full power of silent films, primarily with Kevin Brownlow's lovingly restored version of Abel Gance's *Napoleon* (1927) and King Vidor's *Big Parade* (1925) and *The Crowd* (1928). Silent cinema had been dismissed as a trivial, mannered and overtly melodramatic medium, but seeing these silent masterpieces with full orchestral accompaniment, one can imagine the impact they would have had on audiences 60 years before, the sort of impact they would have had on the young Alfred Hitchcock.

British cinema stood in awe of the innovations and artistic bounds its American counterparts were making. Cinema's first aesthetic landmark came in 1915, when Hitchcock was 16, with D W Griffith's *Birth of a Nation*. Although hindsight

Previous Pages: *If looks could speak . . .* Champagne *(1928).*
Opposite: *The young Hitchcock – already the profile is unmistakable.*

D.W. GRIFFITH'S
IMMORTAL MASTERPIECE

THE BIRTH OF A NATION
WITH SOUND

Above: *A poster for Griffith's historic 1915 film.*
Right: *Silent master D W Griffith.*

reveals the odious racial bigotry of the film – with the Ku Klux Klan portrayed as heroes – it received the sort of acclaim the fledgling medium desperately needed. President Wilson went so far as to refer to it as like 'history written by lightning.'

While American films continued to dominate world cinema, Griffith's career was already in decline, and some of the most interesting cinema was emerging from the postwar chaos of Germany. The film which first drew the world's attention to Germany was *The Cabinet of Dr Caligari* (1919), a chilling, surrealistic film. The sets were revolutionary, relying on distorted perspective and cunning design to convey the madness of one man's mind. In the immediate aftermath of World War I, and prior to the rise of Hitler, German cinema exercised a strong influence on the young Hitchcock; directors such as Robert Wiene, Fritz Lang and Ernst Lubitsch were beginning the work which would later bring them international recognition.

Hitchcock's artistic bent paid off when he read that the American studio Paramount (then known as Famous Players Lasky) was opening a branch in Islington, London, near where he lived. Hitchcock had by then been inducted into the drawing department of Henley's, and applied for a job in the title department, after submitting some of his drawings. He was engaged, and went on to become head of the department. There was a sense of freewheeling adventurism in film in those days; Hitchcock recalled that it was the captions which dictated the type of film, so if a potboiling melodrama was not well received on its initial showings, the captions were re-written in a humorous vein, and the film swiftly reissued as a comedy! In these days of inflated budgets, it is hard to conceive of films being made on such a shoestring and in such a cavalier fashion.

Paramount's Islington studios were not the success originally envisaged, and British companies leased the studios early in the 1920s. Hitchcock applied for the job of Assistant Director, roughly equivalent to that of Assistant Stage Manager in repertory theater. This somewhat menial position gave him invaluable experience of filmmaking from every angle – scenic design, editing, scriptwriting and directing. Hitchcock wrote captions for a number of films by Scottish actor Donald Crisp, a versatile young man who emigrated to America at the turn of the century, and was assistant to the great D W Griffith on *Birth of a Nation*.

Halfway through the 1920s a paltry five percent of films shown in Britain were made in the country, and the export potential was pitiful. A number of creative filmmakers in Britain were depressed about the virtual nonexistence of an indigenous film industry, and some of them arrived at the Islington studios. Two such talents were Michael Balcon and Victor Saville, who made a film called *Woman to Woman* (1923), with Hitchcock as screenwriter, assistant director and art director. Balcon remembered the young Hitchcock's 'passion for films and his eagerness to learn.' The film went on to become one of the most successful made in Britain

Michael Balcon (above) *and Victor Saville* (below), *two of Hitchcock's early mentors at Islington. The young Hitchcock worked with them on* Woman to Woman *(1923).*

Below: *In headphones, Ernst Lubitsch, another of Hitchcock's early influences.*

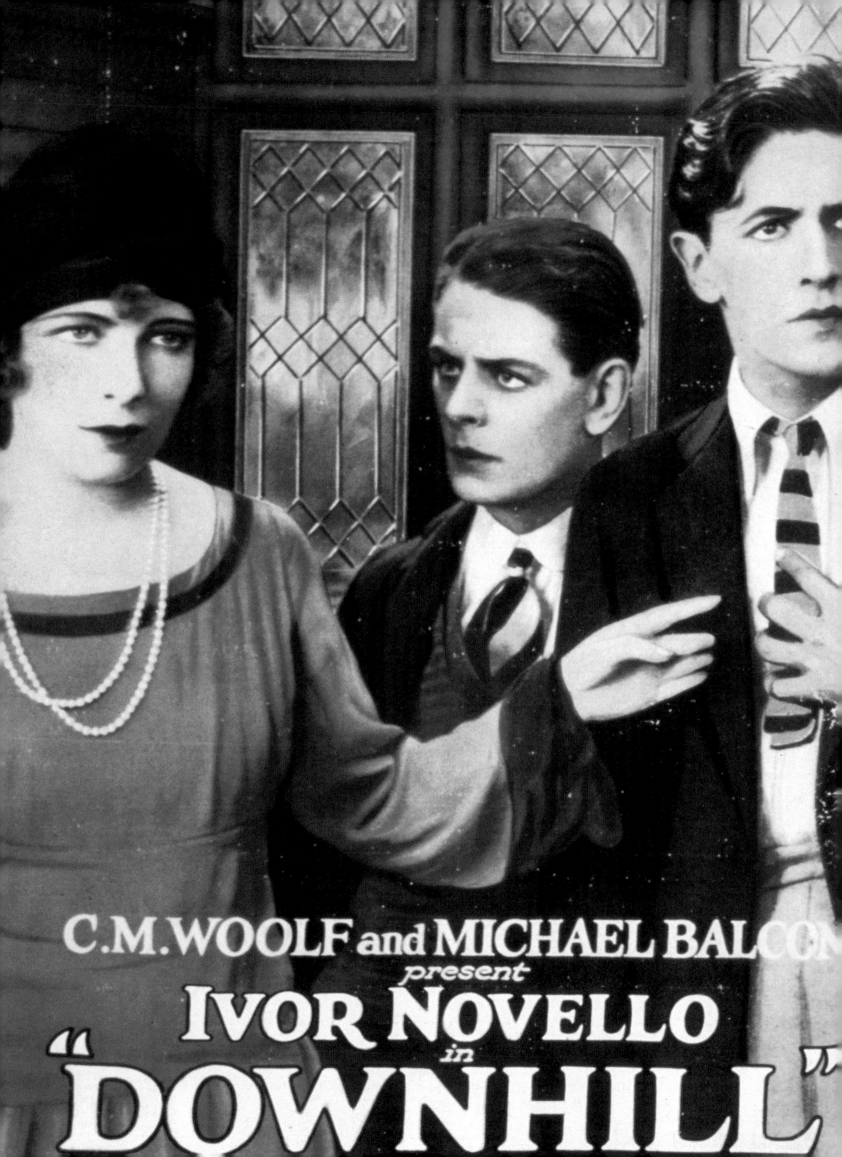

C.M. WOOLF and MICHAEL BALCON

present

IVOR NOVELLO

in

"DOWNHILL"

Above: Woman To Woman *(1923) and (*right*)*
Passionate Adventure *(1924), early Islington*
films for which Hitchcock was joint scriptwriter,
art director and assistant director.
Opposite: *Publicity poster for* Downhill *(1927).*

Above: The Prude's Fall *(1925), on which Hitchcock learned his craft.*
Below: *A rare early photograph of Hitchcock and Alma Reville, soon to become his wife.*

Above: *Spectacular Hitchcock set design for* The Blackguard *(1925)*.

during the 1920s, and even achieved quite a healthy showing at the important US box office. Hitchcock had in fact started work as a director on a film called *Number 13* (1922), a two-reeler which was never completed, but his experience was growing and *Woman to Woman* had a far more important impact on his life than being given the reins of a feature film to handle.

It was during the making of this film that Hitchcock first met his wife to be, Alma Reville. She was credited as editor on *Woman to Woman* but over the next half century was to be Hitchcock's permanent companion, script advisor and confessor. Hitchcock proposed on a cross-Channel ferry during a violent storm, reasoning that Alma's resistance would be so low owing to her seasickness that she could not refuse him! They were married in December 1926 at Brompton Oratory, and had one child, a daughter Patricia, born in 1928.

While at Islington, Hitchcock worked as a general assistant on a number of silent productions, including *The Prude's Fall* (1924), *Passionate Adventure* (1924) and *The Blackguard* (1925). None of them is particularly noteworthy and each took about one month to film. Hitchcock remembered only *Woman to Woman* with any affection. Eventually Balcon asked if Hitchcock would care to direct a film himself, and the result was *The Pleasure Garden* (1925), the first film to bear the now-legendary credit 'Directed by Alfred Hitchcock.'

Immediately prior to his directorial debut, Hitchcock had travelled with Balcon to the influential UFA Studios in Berlin, and watched the great F W Murnau work on the silent masterpiece *The Last Laugh* (1925), with Emil Jannings. The young Hitchcock watched spellbound as the irascible but brilliant Murnau clambered around the massive sets and noted how he extracted such a touching performance from Jannings. It was to prove a fascinating introduction into the craft of making movies, although the trip was fraught with financial difficulties and Hitchcock was rather disconcerted by the frank sexuality of Weimar Germany.

Hitchcock admitted that by the age of 23 he had never been out with a woman, never taken alcohol, and was completely ignorant of the opposite sex. But his sheltered life was coming to an end; when Alma accepted his proposal of marriage, a partnership was forged the effects of which were to leave their mark on cinema for the next 50 years. For while it was Alfred Hitchcock's name which sold a film, the omniscient hand of Alma oversaw initial script development and followed the film through shooting and postproduction. It was Alma for example who noticed that Janet Leigh's body twitched for two frames after her murder in *Psycho*. It was such a fine attention to detail which made the Hitchcocks such a formidable creative partnership, and together they went on to work on the film which is recognized as the first 'authentic Hitchcock.'

Inset: *A difference of opinion in* The Blackguard.
Main picture: *A scene from the first film to bear the credit 'Directed by Alfred Hitchcock,'* The Pleasure Garden *(1925)*.

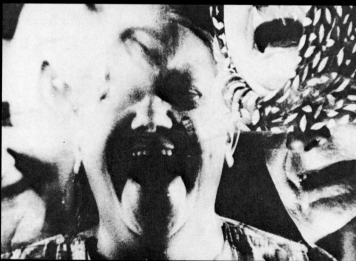

Top: *Filming Emil Jannings in F W Murnau's silent classic* The Last Laugh *(1925).*
Above: *An example of Murnau's innovative montage technique from* The Last Laugh.
Right: *Hitchcock at work on his second film,* The Mountain Eagle *(1926). Sadly no prints of this film survive. To his right is Alma, who became his wife in December that year.*

Above: *Hitchcock's first screen appearance, in* The Lodger.
Top: *A scene from* The Lodger *(1926), 'the first true Hitchcock movie.'*
Left: *Ivor Novello starred in* The Lodger.

The Lodger: A Story of the London Fog (1926) is based on a novel by Mrs Belloc Lowndes. A variant of the Jack the Ripper legend, it was set in the London fog of Hitchcock's youth. Hitchcock saw the play *Who Is He?* (based on the Belloc Lowndes novel) and realized the cinematic possibilities. The film evokes the high Victorian era: the capital is swathed in fog, hansom cabs (no doubt bearing Holmes and Watson on another urgent errand) click through the streets, the low moan of foghorns drifts in from the river, and through the night stalks a madman intent on the horrific murder of prostitutes.

The original novel centers on a boarding house, with the landlady suspecting that her new, sinister lodger is the Ripper. Hitchcock was keen to 'cast against type' and decided on matinee idol Ivor Novello as the likely murderer. Novello had already established himself as a popular song and revue writer in the Noel Coward vein, and his 'Keep The Home Fires Burning' had become virtually the anthem of World War I. Novello's lean good looks saw him established as a box-office attraction. He appeared in his own adaptation of *The Lodger* which was made as a talkie in 1932, but his version is less well known than Hitchcock's. Novello's appeal to women was never undermined by his homosexuality and, despite Hitchcock's avowed prudery, the two men got on well during filming.

Right: *Ivor Montagu was brought in to edit* The Lodger, *helping it to become the first Hitchcock triumph.*
Below: Downhill *(1927), which reunited Hitchcock with Ivor Novello.*

Above: *Scene from* Easy Virtue *(1927), which was based on a play by Noel Coward.*

The Lodger is recognized as being the first authentic Hitchcock; the hallmarks of subtlety which were to characterize Hitchcock's later work are already apparent. The film's most famous scene comes when the landlady and her family's suspicions about their lodger's true identity come close to breaking point. In one classic shot, which bursts through the restrictions of silent cinema, Hitchcock shows Novello pacing to and fro in his room on a glass floor, which means that the landlady downstairs and the audience can share their suspicions about his true motives.

Hitchcock told Truffaut that he regarded *The Lodger* as his 'first picture.' Indeed, the film bears Hitchcock's hallmarks – the innocent man, pursued and condemned, striving to prove his innocence; the technical excellence; the growing suspense and ultimate revelations. The influence of the UFA Studios on Hitchcock and his admiration for the work of the German silent directors is obvious in the stylized settings, the dense atmosphere, the mastery of light and shade and the assured cutting.

Aside from establishing his name as a young English director to be reckoned with, *The Lodger* marked Hitchcock's first appearance on screen. In later years Hitchcock's cameo appearances became as much a part of his films as the plot. Somewhat ironically, his debut in *The Lodger* happened by chance – the screen had to be filled with extras for a news-room scene, and Hitchcock was simply there to swell the numbers (he also can be glimpsed near the end of the film, as an onlooker when Ivor Novello is arrested). He told Truffaut: 'Later on, it became a superstition and eventually a gag. But by now it's a rather troublesome gag, and I'm very careful to show up in the first five minutes so as to let people look at the rest of the movie with no further distraction.'

There was a problem before the finished film was released. The distributors felt that it was too highbrow and a young 'infiltrator' into the nascent British film industry, Ivor Montagu, was asked in to re-edit the film and make it a tighter commercial prospect. Montagu's first reaction to the film he saw was that 'all Hitch's special qualities stood out raw: the narrative skill, the ability to tell the story and create the tension in graphic combination, and the feeling for London scenes and characters.' But Montagu and the film's producers felt that the silent film was too wordy. Montagu cut down the captions from around 400 to 80 which, along with judicious editing, helped tighten the pace. *The Lodger* was threatened with being shelved despite Novello's popularity, and Montagu's editing certainly helped it gain a commercial release, and led to its ultimate popular response. Hitchcock himself was unhappy that the film had been taken out of his hands. Ultimately though it was a satisfactory decision, for without Montagu's work *The Lodger* could well have remained on a shelf, thereby denying the public access to Hitchcock's work. It left an impression on the young Hitchcock though and his subsequent career saw him striving to gain complete control over his films.

In the meantime, *The Lodger* established Hitchcock's reputation. On its release it was hailed as 'the best British production ever made.' The film enjoyed considerable success in both Britain and Europe, where its Germanic feel no doubt aided its appeal. At the age of 27, newly married and with a successful film under his already portly belt, Alfred Hitchcock had arrived as a filmmaker.

Hitchcock swiftly followed with *The Mountain Eagle* (1926), the only one of his films of which a print no longer survives. It was a pot-boiling melodrama with the location inexplicably switched from Kentucky to the Austrian Tyrol; to complicate matters further, no one was able to speak English. Hitchcock was happy to forget this film.

But the *auteur* so beloved of later critics was still hidebound to the studio. The following films, *Downhill* (1927) and *Easy Virtue* (1927), were fillers. Hitchcock recalled that a couple of melodramatic touches – the boy starting his downhill slide being shown going on a down escalator – were well received at the time, but aged badly. He recalled with fondness a scene in *Downhill* depicting the seduction of a young man by an older woman, and the young man's reaction as the dawn's early light revealed just how much older the woman was! Interestingly, the play on which the film was based was written by Ivor Novello.

Opposite and above: *Scenes from* The Ring *(1927), one of Hitchcock's own silent favorites.*

Easy Virtue was based on a play by Novello's contemporary, Noel Coward. This silent film had little of merit except for Hitchcock's fond memory of a crucial dialogue between two lovers being relayed by the expressions of a telephone operator who connects them, with veteran silent-screen actress Bessie Love as the operator. Hitchcock claimed that the film contained his worst title ever: 'Following a well-publicized divorce, the famous actress involved stands outside the courtroom and peremptorily instructs the banks of photographers "Shoot – there's nothing left to kill!"'

'You might say that after *The Lodger, The Ring* was the next Hitchcock picture,' the director told Truffaut in 1966. This 1927 film was another assignment of which Hitchcock remained fond. He depicted the boxer hero's rise in the world by showing his name first appearing at the bottom of posters, and through the seasons rising to the top of the bill; a commonplace device half a century later, this was quite an innovation at the time. Aside from *The Lodger, The Ring* stands as one of the most talked about Hitchcock films from the silent period. Hitchcock felt that sly touches such as having the hero's assistant pulling out a brand new 'Round 2' card, (the hero was 'One Round Jack'), were lost on the silent audiences. The film also contained a vignette of circus side-show freaks, a scene which was to recur in *Saboteur* (1942). some 15 years later.

Above: The Farmer's Wife *(1928) was also adapted from a successful stage play. However. it remains an unmemorable Hitchcock film of the period and is rarely shown.*

During 1928 Hitchcock directed three films, *The Farmer's Wife*, *Champagne* and *The Manxman*, but with little real enthusiasm. Although Hitchcock felt that *Champagne* had certain redeeming features, particularly the archetypal drunk-at-sea sequence, he told Truffaut that the only interest of *Manxman* is that 'it was my last silent one.'

Hitchcock was obviously aware that he was in at the beginning of a new era in the history of cinema – the advent of sound. As an innovator Hitchcock could not wait to try out the new talking pictures. However, he retained a fondness for the silent era and felt that all potential students of cinema should study film history from the beginning, starting with Méliès and tracing its growth until they were conversant with all technical development right up to the present.

Hitchcock cited D W Griffith as the innovator who 'took the camera away from the proscenium arch . . . and moved it as close as possible to the actors.' In his late sixties Hitchcock berated modern filmmakers as men who made 'photographs of people talking,' yearning for the challenge that silent cinema threw down to its directors. He said, 'I always try to tell a story in the cinematic way, through a succession of shots, and bits of film in-between. It seems unfortunate that with the arrival of sound, the motion picture, overnight, assumed a theatrical form.' While it is impossible to imagine

Left: *Surreal scene from the effervescent* Champagne *(1928)*.
Below: *A rugged Isle of Man location (actually Cornwall) from* The Manxman *(1928)*.

cinema today without sound, one can appreciate the nostalgia for the form of silent pictures that veterans like Hitchcock retained.

Today, as we approach the end of the 20th century, there are few directors around who can recall the thrill or the purity of silent films; those of any quality survived the transition from silence to sound, but it is easy to appreciate their affection for the medium which *had* to tell a story through visual representation. The poetry of Griffith, the exuberance of Eisenstein, the spectacle of Gance, all are enshrined as pure examples of silent cinema. But as one keen to pursue the still young medium to its limits, Alfred Hitchcock was like a child on Christmas morning, eager to unwrap the package that came labeled as 'sound cinema.'

Top: The Manxman *(1928) was to be Hitchcock's last silent film.*
Left: *Hitchcock (front, far left) with Betty Balfour to his left together with other studio staff during filming of* Champagne.

The shadowy Verloc menacing his wife in Sabotage *(1936).*

THE BRITISH CLASSICS

It began with *The Jazz Singer* (1927) when vaudevillian Al Jolson instructed technicians on the set, 'Hang around, you ain't heard nothin' yet!' Appositely these are the first words spoken on the cinema screen. There had of course been attempts at marrying sound and vision before, but with the 'all singing, all talking' *The Jazz Singer* Warner Brothers offered an irresistible combination – the human voice *synchronized* with moving pictures. It had taken just over 30 years, but the residue of silent films was dispatched in as many minutes; when the future was seen to be that of talkies the film industry geared itself to a transition the scale of which it has never again had to face. Despite all the gimmickry which has since attached itself like a virus to cinema – Smell-O-Rama, Feelies, 3-D – the transition from silent to sound was the one resounding change with which cinema has had to cope in its 90-year history, and Hitchcock was right there supervising its emergence in British films. For many, it spelled the end of their careers: stars whose voices could not make the transition, directors whose styles were too closely married to the purely visual, studios who felt that talkies were a three-minute wonder. But to those like Hitchcock who had, literally, grown up with film, it offered an exciting and exhilarating challenge.

Studio heads, the money men, were predictably nervous about the introduction of talkies, hesitant about committing themselves to the new novelty. Hitchcock was already committed to *Blackmail* (1929). The film was based on a successful play by Charles Bennett which Hitchcock saw during its London run; he was particularly impressed by the leading actress Tallulah Bankhead, with whom he worked on *Lifeboat* in 1943. Hitchcock adapted the play in conjunction with Bennett, and anticipated that the producers might eventually want an all sound picture and worked on it with that in mind.

'Well, we finished earlier tonight than I expected' is not the screen's most memorable line, but it does merit a footnote in the history of British cinema as the first line spoken in Britain's first full-length talking picture. Strangely, *Blackmail* fares less well than some of Hitchcock's early, silent work. You can sense the director's eagerness to experiment with the new medium, but the overall effect of the 92-minute film – long for those days – is curiously stilted and remote. Hitchcock made the film as a silent picture, but anticipated that the demand for sound would override the original conception. This duality is apparent in the finished film which, over half a century later, remains stilted. The actual *sound* of the film is unconvincing, and only in the obviously sound-staged sequences does any degree of naturalness materialize. This is further complicated by the inability of the leading lady to speak English! Anny Ondra, the attractive blonde German-Czech actress, was cast when *Blackmail* was to be a largely silent film and during the transition it became apparent that her accent was so impenetrable and her command of the language so minimal that she would have to be dubbed. Hitchcock recruited the English actress Joan Barry to stand on set and read the dialogue while Miss Ondra mimed along. It obviously was not the most satisfactory of arrangements and it is a testament to the abilities of Anny Ondra that she manages to convey any rapport with her character at all.

The quality of acting throughout the film is generally poor. John Longden, making his film debut as Frank, the detective, is hidebound by conventional stage techniques, and is chillingly stilted and awkward. (His ability as a film actor was further tested in 1930 when he starred in *Atlantic*, performing

Opposite: *Original poster from Hitchcock's* Blackmail *(1929), Britain's first full-length sound film.*
Above: *Anny Ondra with the murder weapon from* Blackmail.

with all the zeal of a drugged puppy, a performance that frequently turns up on 'Movie Worsts' programs.)

However *Blackmail* is not without its moments. The film's most famous sequence has Hitchcock lovingly and effectively experimenting with the new sound medium: on returning home from stabbing her seducer, Anny Ondra undergoes a gruelling breakfast with her parents and nosy neighbor, and Hitchcock brilliantly revolves the whole scene around the word 'knife.' The neighbor is heard revelling in the gruesome details of the murder, 'A knife is a difficult thing to handle . . . knife isn't a very British thing . . .,' until Hitchcock isolates her speech into a drone, singling out *knife*. The suspense is sustained when Ondra's father asks her to cut a slice of bread and adds 'Careful, you might cut somebody with that!' Even today, there is a delight in seeing and hearing Hitchcock playing with the possibilities of sound for the first time.

The narrative development of the film is effectively handled by Hitchcock, making excellent use of locations. The London he depicts near the film's beginning owes more to Charles Dickens than to the 20th century. Hitchcock makes obeisance to the German silent cinema he so admired with effective set designs and lovingly photographed black-and-white shots which play with light. After committing the murder, the girl moves like the robot in Fritz Lang's recently

Above: *Hitchcock (with book) in* Blackmail, *one of his first screen appearances.*
Below: *An awesome scene from Fritz Lang's futuristic* Metropolis *(1926).*

rereleased *Metropolis* (1926). Hitchcock's touch of genius is revealed in her recurrent sighting of outstretched hands (a traffic policeman's, a sleeping tramp's) which bring back the sight of the murdered artist's hand. Hitchcock again delights in *using* sound – a smooth transition is achieved when what the viewer assumes is Ondra screaming turns out to be the landlady discovering the corpse.

The film has its fair share of in-jokes; Ondra talks to her boyfriend about the authenticity of a new film *Fingerprints* they are to see, and comments 'It's bound to be authentic, I hear they got a real criminal to direct it!' The artist/seducer-of-Ondra is a suave lounge lizard in the Noel Coward vein. Coward was exactly the same age as Hitchcock and came from a similar middle-class background but he was everything Hitchcock was not: self-assured, homosexual, confident and slim! His plays were beginning to achieve notoriety, and one detects a hint of envy in Hitchcock's portrayal of the artist, elegantly sitting playing the piano, confident of his ability to seduce his victim.

Blackmail's climax comes with a chase through the British Museum, another example of Hitchcock's keenness to play around with unlikely locations in order to achieve the desired effect. The light was not sufficiently good to shoot actually in the Museum, so Hitchcock cunningly adopted the Schufftan Process. This process re-creates certain scenes by the use of

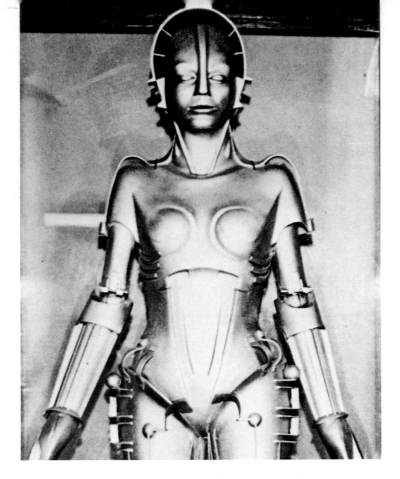

Above: *The climactic British Museum chase scene from* Blackmail, *which borrowed processes pioneered in* Metropolis.
Left: *Imaginative robot from Lang's classic,* Metropolis.

mirrors and transparencies and had been brilliantly used in *Metropolis* a few years before. For all its faults, *Blackmail* is of course of interest to the Hitchcock *aficionado*, not least for the characters and locations which crop up again later in his career. The factual depiction of the process of arrest with which the film opens recurs in later Hitchcock films such as *The Paradine Case* and *The Wrong Man*. Tracy, the seedily suave blackmailer played by Donald Calthrop, is a none-too-distant relative of Captain Lesgate, played by Anthony Dawson in *Dial M For Murder* (1953); and the final scene of *Blackmail* has Anny Ondra staring from a room in Scotland Yard across the river to County Hall, the location to which Hitchcock would return for the opening of *Frenzy* 43 years later.

Blackmail's distinction as the first British sound film was heralded by the original poster thus: 'See and Hear our Mother Tongue as it should be – SPOKEN!' Hitchcock's authorized biographer John Russell Taylor wrote: 'Though Hitch was to have his reverses and thin periods during the next few years, there was never again after *Blackmail* any danger of him being ignored or discounted.'

With two hits in the shape of *The Lodger* and *Blackmail* behind him, Hitchcock was established as an important young British director, forever keen to experiment, having proved his innate mastery of the medium. He was also in the process of establishing his reputation as 'The Master of Suspense,' but he was still beholden to the whims and production necessities of his employers. Like the production line facilities of the Hollywood Studios at their peak, British International Pictures had a certain quota of films to meet – one of which was the lamentable *Elstree Calling* (1930), the studio's response to the then-popular Hollywood revues. Hitchcock was contracted to film a couple of sequences with the popular cockney comedian Gordon Harker, with whom he had worked earlier on *The Ring*, but he later dismissed the subsequent film as 'of no interest whatsoever.' Harker turned up as the popular radio detective Inspector Hornleigh in a light-hearted trio of films in the late 1930s, examples of the

direction Hitchcock could have taken in his career had not Hollywood beckoned.

With cinema established as *the* mass-media entertainment of the era, the studios' demand for new films was insatiable. Plays were often adapted for film, having proven themselves in pulling audiences to theaters, and Hitchcock was the unlikely choice of director for the film adaptation of Sean O'Casey's successful play *Juno and the Paycock*, which he filmed with the Irish Players in 1930. One reason for his dislike of the end result was that Hitchcock saw it as a return to the proscenium-arch type of filmmaking, from which he felt Griffith had freed directors a decade before. But the finished film was well received, and Hitchcock's relationships with his largely Irish cast and with O'Casey himself were cordial.

Hitchcock's final film of 1930 saw him back on home ground. *Murder* was adapted by the devoted Alma from a play by Clemence Dane. It is a thin, melodramatic piece about a young actress who is accused of murdering a friend, and only thanks to the dedication of one of the jurors is it revealed that the murderer is none other than the actress's fiancé. Hitchcock called it 'one of the rare whodunnits' he made, and expressed a distaste for the genre because 'they're rather like a jigsaw or a crossword puzzle. No emotion. You simply wait to find out who committed the murder.'

Hitchcock particularly enjoyed working with the elegant Herbert Marshall, who played the juror. A decade later Marshall turned in a memorable performance as the smoothly sinister villain in Hitchcock's *Foreign Correspondent*. Technically the film posed problems, as the studios were still coming to terms with the complexities of sound, and for one scene a 30-piece orchestra was required on set to play the musical accompaniment, which was then directly recorded on to the soundtrack. *Murder* was conceived as an Anglo-German production, so the film was shot side by side in English and German, with two entirely separate casts! Although *Murder* was extremely tied to the theater (there are numerous examples of a 'play within a play' in the film)

Above: *Hitchcock on set for* Juno and the
Paycock *(1930); Alma, with whom he adapted
O'Casey's play, is by the fireplace.*
Right: *The Irish Players in a scene from the
finished film.*

Above: *Herbert Marshall (right) in* Murder *(1930), an imaginative whodunnit.*
Below: *John Galsworthy, whose play* The Skin Game *Hitchcock adapted for film in 1931.*

Hitchcock lent it a fluency and pace which was lacking from his earlier theatrical ventures.

Hitchcock perforce returned to filmed plays in 1931 with *The Skin Game*, an adaptation of John Galsworthy's play. Again this was foisted on him, and for it he retained no affection. He felt even less affection for the author, particularly after one dreadful dinner with the Galsworthys.

Rich and Strange, made later in 1932, was an uncharacteristically humorous Hitchcock. It was based on an original script by Alma and inspired by events which overtook the Hitchcocks during a holiday, culminating with a trip to a Paris bordello, which left Mr and Mrs Hitchcock marooned, two innocents abroad. Hitchcock was then assigned, and dutifully undertook, a film called *Number Seventeen* (1932), again based on a stage play. He produced *Lord Camber's Ladies* (1932), a 'quota quickie' made to appease the studio.

The oddest example from this period was *Waltzes From Vienna* (1933), adapted from a play by Guy Bolton, P G Wodehouse's long-time collaborator. With music by older and younger Strausses, the film starred Jessie Matthews, then very much the doyenne of British musicals. The colorful, frothy musical was quite at odds with the reputation which Hitchcock had established as the director of taut, efficient and psychologically effective thrillers. Indeed Hitchcock himself was keen to film Dennis Wheatley's first novel *The Forbidden Territory*, which was published in 1933, but the studio insisted he tackle *Waltzes From Vienna*, which the director felt was his creative nadir. However, Hitchcock was always a consummate craftsman and, however much he disliked the property he was working on, he always managed to deliver a competent, and at times a brilliant, film.

It was again thanks to Michael Balcon that Hitchcock's flagging reputation was saved. Balcon had given Hitchcock his first break as a director in Islington. They met while Hitchcock was finishing *Waltzes From Vienna*, and Balcon discovered that Hitchcock was keen to film a screenplay he had obtained. Balcon eventually bought the screenplay for £500 and it became *The Man Who Knew Too Much* (1934).

With *Waltzes* finished and generally well received he braced himself for a make or break effort. Hitchcock was still only in his early thirties, but had already established himself as potentially one of the country's finest directors. Happy to be working together again, Balcon and Hitchcock set out to make the film which, once and for all, established the young Hitchcock as 'The Master of Suspense' and launched a career synonymous with style, durability and quality – a career unparalleled in cinema history.

There had been early triumphs with *The Lodger* and *Blackmail*, there had been the pitfalls of *The Skin Game* and *Elstree Calling*, but even these had given Alfred Hitchcock the opportunity to experiment and learn his craft. By the age of 35, Hitchcock was keen to expand and flex his creative muscles.

Left: *A tense moment from the undistinguished* Number Seventeen *(1932)*.
Below: Rich and Strange *(1932); unusually, it was based on an original screenplay by Alma*.
Opposite: *The glamorous Jill Esmond in* The Skin Game *(1931)*.

For Hitchcock *The Man Who Knew Too Much* was the turning point. The film's background is the London of his childhood and the climax is directly reminiscent of the 1911 Siege of Sidney Street. A group of anarchists was besieged in a house in an East End slum, led by 'Peter The Painter,' whose body was mysteriously never recovered after the gunmen had been smoked out. Winston Churchill was Home Secretary and authorized the early police use of firearms. The police were held at bay and Churchill commanded the police at the scene. Another onlooker at the scene was a social worker in Stepney at the time – future Labour Prime Minister Clement Attlee.

Even a quarter of a century after the actual events, Hitchcock ran into trouble with the censor over the siege at the end of the film, when the police are carrying firearms. Predictably, Hitchcock ignored this problem. The finished film, which cost a paltry £40,000, was Hitchcock's greatest commercial success to date and also helped establish his name in the United States, bringing it to the attention of the mogul David O Selznick. Interestingly, it is the only one of his films which Hitchcock chose to remake; in 1956 James Stewart and Doris Day played the roles created by Leslie Banks and Edna Best. The story concerns a couple of British tourists in Switzerland who witness a murder. The dying man tells them of a plot to assassinate a leading diplomat in London and, to ensure the couple's silence, the plotters kidnap their daughter. Together, they manage to thwart the assassination and rescue their daughter after a shoot-out with the kidnappers.

The film's most famous moment is the foiled assassination during a concert at the Royal Albert Hall. Like so many of Hitchcock's films, there is one scene which lingers and, breaking the scene down, it is easy to see why. It is a typically wry touch that the actual assassination is to take place in such a public setting as a concert at the Royal Albert Hall, the apogee of high Victorian culture and respectability. To ensure the audience's 'collaboration,' Hitchcock shows the murderers rehearsing the shooting in time with a recording of the concert. This ensures that when the cymbals crash at the crescendo, allowing the diplomat to be killed with one shot, the cinema audience is virtually an accomplice.

The plot is eventually foiled by Edna Best, but the sustained intensity of the sequence is unmatched. There is also a taut sequence when Leslie Banks undergoes interrogation in a dentist's surgery, neatly prefacing John Schlesinger's painful scene with Olivier and Hoffman in *Marathon Man* (1976). With hindsight, Hitchcock professed that the remake was his favorite version, rather pompously declaring that 'the first version is the work of a talented amateur and the second was made by a professional.'

The Man Who Knew Too Much was a generally happy experience for Hitchcock. Alma, of course, collaborated on the screenplay. Additional dialogue was contributed by a young Welsh playwright Emlyn Williams, whose best-known play, the psychological thriller *Night Must Fall*, was filmed in 1937 with some Hitchcock-like touches. *The Man Who Knew Too Much* also gave Hitchcock the opportunity to work with Peter Lorre, who was making his British film debut. Lorre had just fled from Germany following Hitler's rise to power and had established himself as a major cinematic force with his chilling performance as a child murderer in Fritz Lang's disturbing *M*.

Below: *Crucial scene from* Waltzes from Vienna *(1933) – 'a musical without music' according to Hitchcock.*

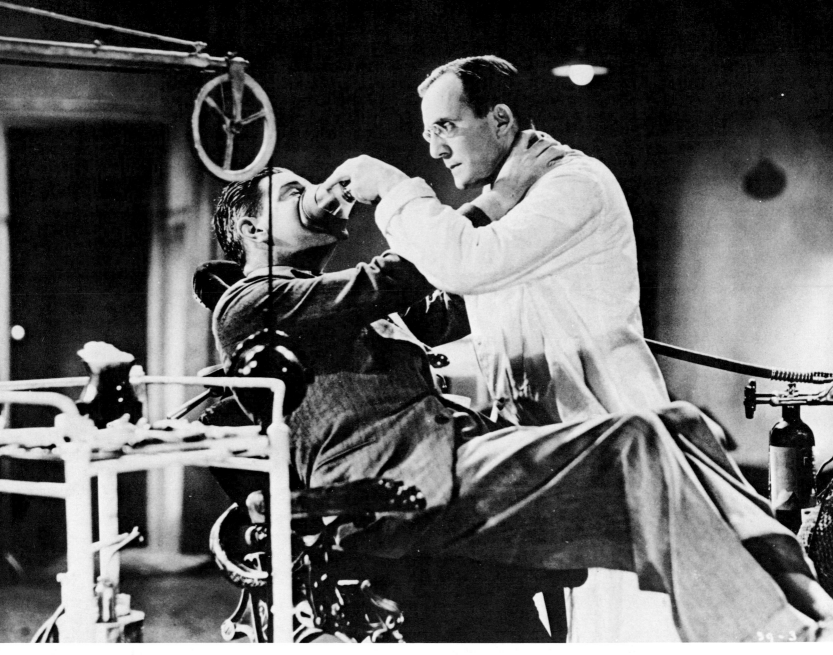

Top, left and above: *Three scenes from* The Man Who Knew Too Much *(1934) which Hitchcock remade in 1956, with little improvement.*

Talking to Truffaut about his original version of the film, especially about the cymbal sequence, Hitchcock made a valuable point: 'I've often found that a suspense situation is weakened because the action is not sufficiently clear. For instance, if two actors should happen to be wearing similar suits, the viewer can't tell one from the other; if the location is not clearly established, the viewer may be wondering where the action is taking place. And if a crucial scene unfolds while he is trying to figure these things out, its emotional impact is dissipated.' It is an important point, not only in considering Hitchcock's own career, but in evaluating the thriller/suspense genre overall. Throughout many of his conversations, particularly with Truffaut, Hitchcock is at pains to consider the impact of a scene on the audience. Many filmmakers tend to ignore their audiences altogether, particularly during the exposition or dénouement of the plot. Many crucial scenes today seem to take place at airports, against blaring soundtracks, or are mumbled into distant microphones, thereby rendering much of the plot inaudible. Such devices suggest a contempt for the wider audience, with a film aimed at an elite who have the time and facilities constantly to re-examine and evaluate such scenes. Part of Hitchcock's perennial appeal as a popular filmmaker is his respect for his audience. He always made sure they were in receipt of all the information necessary to ensure their rapt attention to crucial plot developments.

On the release of *The Man Who Knew Too Much* in 1934, Hitchcock entered his golden period of British films. Despite his self-confessed reluctance to tackle familiar novels for the screen, disliking the need to compress while taking one art form and trying to turn it into another, Hitchcock could not resist the challenge of John Buchan's archetypal World War I thriller *The 39 Steps*. Hitchcock had long admired Buchan's work, particularly his 'understatement of a highly dramatic idea,' and was also keen to film the novelist's *Greenmantle*. Buchan's no-nonsense prose and punchy narratives were highly popular between the wars. His top-drawer heroes were notably evoked by Alan Bennett in *40 Years On*: '...

whatsoever is best in England I take to be the Breed. That exclusive club, whose members are the very pith and sinew of this island. You may run across them in the Long Room at Lord's, or dining alone at White's. Once met, you will always know them, for their hand is firm and their eye is clear. ...'

Buchan's plots still make exciting reading, but the anti-Semitism which runs throughout his books is unpalatable today; in mitigation however, it is no more pronounced than that of many upper class Englishmen of the day. The appeal of Buchan's work has seen *The 39 Steps* filmed twice since Hitchcock's now-classic version. A dreary version was made with Kenneth More in 1958, and the 1978 film starred Robert Powell as the hapless Richard Hannay. This rendering restored the film to its original 1914 setting, and boasted a stellar cast of British actors (including Eric Porter, David Warner and Timothy West) and a cliff-hanging climax on the face of Big Ben which was worthy of Hitchcock at the peak of his form.

Hitchcock added much to Buchan's novel, thereby helping make his the definitive version: Carroll and Donat handcuffed together, the crofter scene with Laurie and Ashcroft and the music hall climax. In the dedication to his book, Buchan speaks of his fondness for 'that elementary type of tale which Americans call the "dime novel" ... the romance where the incidents defy the probabilities and march just inside the borders of the possible.' However, sadly, Hitchcock could not work in the little sequence from the original novel where the hero tosses a hunting knife into the air and catches it between his lips. Hitchcock toyed with the idea of showing a conference of spies – all 39 of them – each with a different walk, thereby showing the 39 steps.

Buchan's ripping yarn centers on his famous hero Richard Hannay. Recently returned from South Africa, and fretting at the tedium of life in London compared to the sweep of the veldt, Hannay is mistakenly accused of a murder which, being a founder member of the 'Breed,' needless to say he did not commit. He is pursued to Scotland, evades capture by both the villains and the police, and only manages to survive by denouncing the villains in a nail-biting climax at a music hall. *The 39 Steps* is one of the vintage films of Hitchcock's British period, containing many of his hallmarks: an innocent man falsely accused is pursued by both murderers and police, and earnestly tries to convince a cool and beautiful girl of his innocence. It also contains a number of classic Hitchcock set-pieces and benefits from a gallery of strong performances. Robert Donat excels as Hannay, and was indeed to have starred in *Sabotage* for Hitchcock but a serious attack of his recurrent asthma (which ultimately killed him in 1958) meant that he was unable to appear.

Hitchcock and Donat got on well together, even after the star's infamous introduction to his co-star Madeleine Carroll. In a letter Donat recalled that they were handcuffed together for an hour (later biographies say the pair were handcuffed uncomfortably all day). 'For nearly an hour, Madeleine and I shared this enforced companionship . . . so we talked of our mutual friends, of our ambitions . . .

Left: *One of the first of many awards which Hitchcock was to receive in his lifetime.*
Below: *Robert Donat on the run in the masterly* The 39 Steps *(1934).*

Gradually our reserve thawed as we exchanged experiences. When Hitch saw that we were getting along famously, he extracted the "missing" key from his pocket, released us and said with a satisfied grin "Now that you two know each other we can go ahead."' Donat was afraid of being typecast in thrillers and declined the role of Ashenden in *The Secret Agent*; ill health kept him from the role Michael Redgrave played in *The Lady Vanishes*. In a letter written while preparing for his Oscar-winning role in *Goodbye Mr Chips*, Donat was fulsome in his praise of Hitchcock's handling of him as an actor: 'I rehearsed the (knife) sequence several times in a manner I considered quite adequate. Hitchcock was dissatisfied. "For pity's sake, Bob, don't you realize your life depends on this glance?" I had rehearsed the scene several more times without success when Hitch dispersed all the people standing around and himself demonstrated the sequence for me. Despite his immense weight, Hitchcock is a very balanced and well co-ordinated person. "You see," he said, "you must play it with your heart." For the first time in my life, I tried to feel the situation. That one incident altered my whole outlook.' This testimonial from Donat is at odds with Hitchcock's much publicized disregard for individual performances.

Madeleine Carroll also gives a memorable performance as the first of Hitchcock's unattainable blonde heroines. Godfrey Tearle was another in a growing line of suave villains, and there were memorable cameos from John Laurie and Peggy Ashcroft as the cruel and sinister crofter and his cowed wife.

The film wears so well today, half a century on, because it makes light of many conventional detective story myths, overused even then: the recurrent use of handcuffs, Donat pouring his heart out to a benevolent host only to find him revealed as the villain, the initially disbelieving heroine. The film also makes great play on Hitchcock's fondness for the 'MacGuffin' – the point of the plot that actually has no point, inspired by a story told to him by Angus MacPhail about two men on a train. One asks the other 'What's in that package?' 'It's a MacGuffin.' 'What's a MacGuffin?' 'It's a device for trapping lions in the Scottish Highlands!' 'But there are no lions in the Scottish Highlands . . .' 'Well then, there's no MacGuffin!' This simple plot device was used over and over by Hitchcock during his career: the death of the agent in Hannay's flat at the beginning of *The 39 Steps*; the death of Mr Memory at the end of that film; *all* of *North by Northwest*; the melody whistled during *The Lady Vanishes*; the wine bottles in *Notorious* . . . all are MacGuffins! Hitchcock loved them, they saved many valuable moments of screen time by not having to waste time telling the audience just *why* an item is so important.

There are many enchanting moments in *The 39 Steps*, many of them provided by the enforced handcuffing of Carroll and Donat. Donat's spontaneous bluffing at the local party political meeting is taken one step further in Carol Reed's *The Third Man* (1949) 14 years later, when hoary Western writer Joseph Cotten is seemingly kidnapped but is only being taken to address a British Council meeting on the state of the novel. One scene which recalls Hitchcock's fondness for the dark side of German silent cinema is the scene where Donat seeks sanctuary at Laurie and Ashcroft's cottage. Laurie, best known now for his comedy performances, cuts a chilling figure as the suspicious and tyrannical crofter. Ashcroft plays his terrified wife, who sees Donat as a welcome visitor into their drab lives. The scene is played out with all Hitchcock's directorial skills to the fore, depicting the barrenness and bitterness of their lives together, and the delicious irony of Donat stealing Laurie's coat only to have his life saved by the Bible in the pocket, which stops a bullet!

The film climaxes with a tense though improbable scene, with Mr Memory revealed as the only man who really knows what the 39 Steps are. The character was based on a performer who used to frequent the music halls of Hitchcock's youth who was able to recall thousands of random facts from memory. The film's crucial scene takes place in a music hall, miles away from that temple of high culture – the Royal Albert Hall – which Hitchcock had used so effectively in his previous film. Hitchcock was an avid frequenter of music

Below: *Madeleine Carroll and Robert Donat handcuffed together in* The 39 Steps.

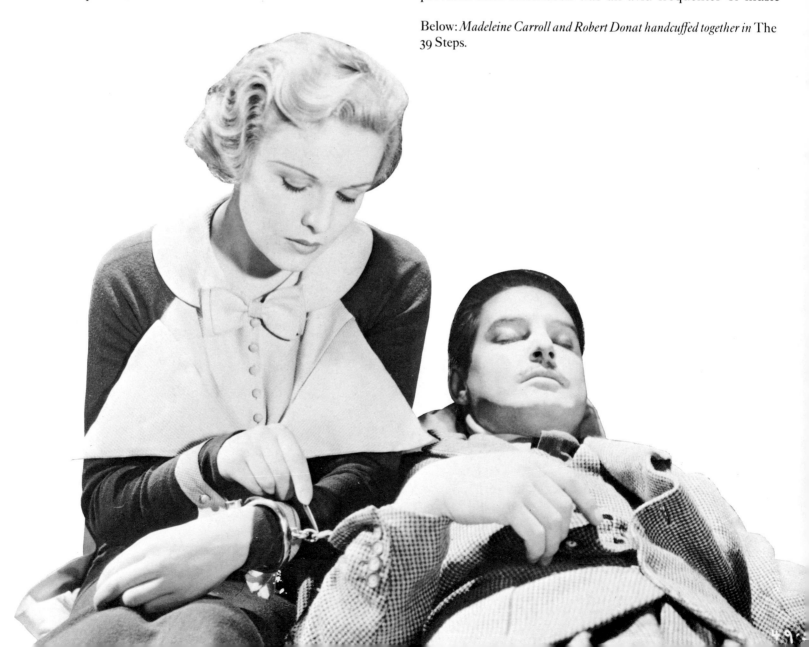

Above: *Police invade the music hall stage at the climax of* The 39 Steps.

halls in his youth and in his later life he lovingly recalled old music-hall songs.

Donat's light touch was a tremendous asset to the film; the notoriously hard-to-please critic of *The Observer*, Caroline Lejeune, wrote: 'Mr Donat, who has never been very well served in the cinema until now, suddenly blossoms out into a romantic comedian of no mean order . . . For the first time on our screen we have the British equivalent of Clark Gable . . . Mr Hitchcock is certainly conscious of it and exploits his new star with all the easy confidence of a local Van Dyke or Capra!'

Already there was a recognizable signature on Alfred Hitchcock's films. He catered to the insatiable demand for films between the wars with ingenious pieces of hokum, brilliantly crafted and ideal for the Golden Age of Cinema, when audiences still yearned for escapism and fantasy. But Hitchcock was too crafty a filmmaker to see his films wholly as escapist; they were all firmly rooted in reality, with identifiable heroes, elegantly compressed into an average 90 minutes of distracting and spellbinding screen time. 'Making a film means, first of all, to tell a story . . . It must be dramatic and human. What is drama, after all, but life with the dull bits cut out?'

From then on, Alfred Hitchcock brilliantly edited out 'the dull bits' and, bolstered by the success of *The 39 Steps*, continued to improve and hone his craft, his mark on a film growing more recognizable with each venture. Soon he would outgrow the still-floundering British cinema, but during the remaining five years he spent making British films he gave cinema some of the most delightful and enchanting moments of screen entertainment.

Above: *W Somerset Maugham, creator of the Ashenden stories on which*
The Secret Agent *(1936) was based.*
Right: *Peter Lorre with Gielgud's shadowy profile in the same film.*

Hitchcock's next project followed swiftly on the heels of
The 39 Steps, and was another adaptation from the works of a
popular English novelist, this time W Somerset Maugham.
Maugham's work was fashionable during the mid-1930s;
both *Rain* and *Of Human Bondage* had been filmed by the time
Hitchcock chose to adapt two of his Ashenden stories for the
screen. Ashenden was a character based on Maugham's own
experiences in the British Intelligence Services during World
War I, and created a prototype for the realistic, self-doubting
'spy' which John le Carré so successfully developed half a
century later. For once, the adaptation did not feature Alma's
name, as she was in the process of adapting Jerome K
Jerome's fable *The Passing of the Third Floor Back* for the
screen, one of her rare commissions not involving her
husband. The final screenplay for *The Secret Agent* (1936) had
a complex genesis. Playwright Campbell Dixon had turned
two of Maugham's Ashenden stories (*The Traitor* and *The
Hairless Mexican*) into a successful play, and this was
fashioned into a screenplay by Charles Bennett, the ubiquitous Ian Hay and the 25-year-old Jesse Lasky Jr.

Despite being well into his stride as a director of sound
films, Hitchcock was always fond of utilizing his original skill
and frequently featured a written title or visual signpost to

Above: *The climactic train crash from* The Secret Agent *which does the reluctant Gielgud's work for him.*
Right: *Mid-30s caricature of the immediately recognizable Hitchcock.*

locate time and place, a trait he retained to the end of his career. Thus in *The Secret Agent* the audience immediately know that they are in the heart of Mayfair, in the third year of World War I and attending a bogus funeral.

Hitchcock chose John Gielgud to play Ashenden. Now celebrated as one of the screen's most distinguished actors, at the time Gielgud was lagging behind his contemporaries Laurence Olivier and Ralph Richardson, who by 1936 had already achieved footholds in the cinema. Gielgud had made only four films prior to *The Secret Agent* and only *The Good Companions* (1932) was regarded as even mildly exceptional. Gielgud mistrusted the medium, and was busy establishing a glowing reputation as the country's leading interpreter of Shakespeare (his Hamlet was the talk of London during the 1936 Season). After filming with Hitchcock during the day, he dashed back to London for performances of *Romeo and Juliet* every evening. It is strange to see Gielgud immersing himself in a full screen role rather than a cameo, but he acquitted himself admirably. His Ashenden is svelte and dashing, all set to play 'The Great Game.' 'Do you love your country?' he is asked by R (a precursor of James Bond's M). 'I've just died for it!' replies Gielgud glibly, referring to his fake funeral which opened the film.

Top: *Young Stevie (Desmond Tester) in* Sabotage *(1936) carrying the fatal time-bomb disguised as a roll of film.*
Above: *A scene from the same film set in Hitchcock's favorite restaurant, featuring John Loder and Sylvia Sidney.*

The Secret Agent continued the happy associations of *The 39 Steps*, reuniting Hitchcock with both Madeleine Carroll and Peter Lorre. Hitchcock revelled in the film's Swiss locations, despite the fact that it was all shot in the studio. He asked himself 'What do they have in Switzerland? They have milk chocolate, they have the Alps, they have village dances and they have lakes!' All these national ingredients were woven into the picture! (These are the very same ingredients which inspired Orson Welles' memorable observation in *The Third Man*: 'In Switzerland, they had brotherly love; they had 500 years of democracy and peace – and what did they produce? The cuckoo clock!')

The film's best scene is the murder of the alleged German spy; Gielgud witnesses Peter Lorre's zealous killing through a telescope, while Hitchcock cuts back to the victim's dog at the hotel reacting to his master's death, a poignant example of the director's craft. Ashenden is a flawed figure, a hero reluctant to carry out his mission. The man whose murder he witnesses and is party to, is in fact innocent, the actual spy dies only accidentally in a train crash at the film's conclusion. Hitchcock particularly enjoyed the set-piece drama in the chocolate factory and the murder of an organist in church. The denouement on the Orient Express is also thrillingly handled, with little asides such as the soldier gloatingly pointing out spies dangling from the gallows in a railway siding.

Despite many positive aspects – Peter Lorre's scene stealing, Hitchcock's obvious affection for Madeleine Carroll, Gielgud's insouciant playing, Robert Young 'cast against type' as the villain – *The Secret Agent* was an unsatisfactory sequel to the driving tour-de-force of *The 39 Steps*. Hitchcock himself said the film 'didn't really succeed. . . . In an adventure drama, your central figure must have a purpose . . . because it's a negative purpose, the film is static – it doesn't move forward.' He also thought there was too much irony and too many twists of fate.

Hitchcock was not alone in his criticisms of the film. Graham Greene, who was then film critic for *The Spectator*, found it dull and inadequate, a travesty of Maugham's fiction. Greene was no fan of Hitchcock's work during those years, he found his adaptation of *The 39 Steps* 'inexcusable,' and wrote that in his films Hitchcock '. . . perfunctorily . . . builds up to these tricky situations (paying no attention on the way to inconsistencies, loose ends, psychological absurdities) and then drops them: they mean nothing: they lead to nothing!' Comparing Hitchcock's film with a 1936 American potboiler, Greene disparagingly wrote: 'The most conventional American melodramas usually have a bite about them; they criticize as well as thrill, and that makes even *One Way Ticket* more convincing and entertaining than the polished fairy tales of Mr Hitchcock!' Even by 1972, when Greene's film criticism was collected together in a single volume, he could not excuse Hitchcock's 'inadequate sense of reality.'

However Greene found much to admire in Hitchcock's next film, *Sabotage* (1936), feeling that 'for the first time, he has really "come off".' Ironically, the film was the most controversial of Hitchcock's British period, specifically because of one scene – the death of a small boy.

Hitchcock told Ken Ferguson in a 1970 interview that this was the biggest mistake he had ever made in a film: 'I made a cardinal error in a film called *Sabotage*, which I made many years ago. In it we had a little boy carrying a bomb which was timed to go off at a certain time. He was carrying the bomb in a parcel across London on a bus. Well, I allowed the bomb to go off, blowing up the bus and killing the little boy. That was a big mistake. I learned that if you have terrific suspense around a bomb you must never let it go off, unless the intended victims find out about it and throw it away in time. But to let it go off, killing someone, that's wrong. You see the audience is looking for relief. They're not relieved!'

Sabotage was based on a story of Joseph Conrad's, confusingly called *The Secret Agent*. Charles Bennett and Ian Hay again collaborated on the screenplay. The story told is of an ostensibly benign cinema manager, Verloc, who is in fact an anarchist saboteur. He lives behind the cinema with his young wife and her younger brother, who is eventually killed when tricked into carrying a time bomb for Verloc. Beside herself with grief, the wife stabs her husband but escapes detection thanks to a convenient explosion in the cinema which destroys Verloc's corpse and the incriminating knife.

The opening is a successful montage which neatly prefaces the narrative: a dictionary definition of 'sabotage,' a bomb planted, the culprit Verloc seen guiltily washing his hands. Also notable is a poignant scene where, as in *Blackmail* seven years earlier, Hitchcock brilliantly builds up to the murder with repetition. While serving dinner the young wife's attention keeps being drawn to her brother's empty seat and she distractedly handles the carving knife which is eventually used to dispatch Verloc.

Above: *The villainous Verloc (Oscar Homolka) plotting further explosions in* Sabotage.

Having Verloc as a cinema owner allows Hitchcock to use a section of Walt Disney's *Silly Symphony* as a counterpoint to the action. The cinema almost becomes a character in its own right, rather like the run-down flea-pit of *The Smallest Show On Earth* (1957) 20 years later.

The aquarium scene pre-empts Orson Welles' *The Lady from Shanghai* (1948) by 12 years; Charles Hawtrey (famous for his appearances in the 'Carry On' films) can be spotted at the end of this sequence. Verloc is castigated by his shadowy boss for 'making London laugh' with his first bomb, and told that it must not happen again, the bombs are to 'take people's minds off events abroad.' Significantly, 1936 was the year of Hitler's invasion of the Rhineland and the outbreak of the Spanish Civil War.

Sabotage lays claim to being Alfred Hitchcock's most obviously autobiographical film. A crucial scene takes place in Simpson's in the Strand, his favorite London restaurant, and Ted, the detective, works undercover in the greengrocers next to the cinema, just the sort of place Hitchcock would remember from his childhood. *Sabotage* reminds us of the danger of film itself – it was illegal to take highly flammable celluloid on public transport; the bomb itself is disguised as a roll of film; and the cinema is a front for Verloc's explosive

activities. The supplier of the explosives is, improbably, a birdseller, and during Verloc's visit to him there is a lingering, almost Dickensian, vignette, when referring to his drudge of a daughter he comments to Verloc tellingly 'We all have our cross to bear.'

The cast is well chosen. Sylvia Sidney, the respected American actress, gives a touching performance as Verloc's wife and Oscar Homolka, in only his second English language film, is outstanding as Verloc. A source of dissatisfaction for Hitchcock was the casting of John Loder as Ted, the detective, and 'friend' of Sylvia Sidney. However, unable to obtain Robert Donat, Hitchcock was saddled with the wooden but enthusiastic Loder. Despite its overtly melodramatic feel, and Hitchcock's callous dismissal of the child, *Sabotage* has sufficient moments spread throughout its 77 minutes to ensure a worthy place in the Hitchcock canon.

With the explosion wrecking the cinema at the end of *Sabotage*, the 'dark period' of Hitchcock's British work came to an end. With the clouds of war looming over Europe posing a very real threat Hitchcock turned to the relief of escapist adventure for his last British films.

Hitchcock was now firmly established on the rollercoaster of fame, with projects coming thick and fast. His next film, *Young and Innocent* (1937), was based on the novel *A Shilling for Candles* by Josephine Tey (probably best known for her novel *The Franchise Affair* which was filmed in 1950). It was released in the United States under the title *A Girl was Young*.

A surprisingly underrated film, *Young and Innocent* contains none of the moral turpitude of his previous work but had no leading players to recommend it. Perhaps this explains why it is so rarely revived now, although it does stand as a prime example of Hitchcock's work in the 1930s.

Derrick de Marney and Nova Pilbeam play a young couple on the run from the police who are pursuing de Marney for a murder he did not commit. It is a slight work, but excels during a couple of spellbinding sequences. For example, the fugitives seek to establish an alibi at Pilbeam's aunt's, arouse her suspicions and are detained during a seemingly innocent game of blind man's buff – again the idea of innocence as a force of menace occurs. There is another engaging scene near the beginning when de Marney, realizing that his lawyer is 'nice' but thoroughly incompetent, effects his escape only to find himself as a spectator at his own trial. But the most memorable moment of this engaging thriller is an exhilarating crane shot at the film's climax. Pilbeam sits at a table in a vast hotel ballroom, scanning the faces of the dancing couples. She is searching for the real murderer, who she knows can be recognized by a facial tic; her audience may feel with some justification that it is impossible to spot a pair of twitching eyes in a crowd of this size. Almost as if challenged, Hitchcock proves that it *is not!* In one bewitching, fluid camera movement, he takes the viewer right up to the top of the set; the camera glides down, past the chandelier, through the crowded lobby into the ballroom, cuts a swathe through the

Opposite: *Alfred Junge's production drawing for the court scene in* Young and Innocent *(1937) and* (top) *the scene as it appeared in the finished film.*
Above: *Nova Pilbeam taking pity on the wrongly accused Derrick de Marney.*
Left: *De Marney and Pilbeam escaping from the police.*

Above: Launder and Gilliat, the talented duo who scripted The Lady Vanishes *(1938).*

milling dancers, and finally settles on the twitching eyes in the blacked-up face of the band's drummer! No wonder that one shot alone took two days to film. In this shot Hitchcock reveals again his inimitable style as a master filmmaker. It is no piece of cinematic legerdemain put in simply to impress critics, but a bravado sleight of hand with which the director rushes the audience to the center of the mystery, while they cling on thrilled by the ride.

The Wheel Spins by Ethel Lina White was the basis of Hitchcock's next film, which was freely adapted for the screen by the already established team of Frank Launder and Sidney Gilliat. By 1938, they were only in their early thirties, but had already achieved credits on *Oh Mr Porter* (1937) and *A Yank at Oxford* (1937), and together they went on to make some of British cinema's most distinguished and idiosyncratic works, including the caustic *Waterloo Road* (1944), *The Rake's Progress* (1945) and the neat thriller *Green for Danger* (1946). From the outline of Mrs White's book, and with a little help from Alma, their screenplay for *The Lady Vanishes* (1938) enshrines it as Hitchcock's most memorable and most thoroughly English work of the 1930s.

The film pairs up Margaret Lockwood and Michael Redgrave as the stars and, immortally, Basil Radford and Naunton Wayne as two cricket-mad passengers. Margaret Lockwood was already a veteran film performer – by her

mid-twenties she had appeared in some 18 films, although her real success lay in the future with the Gainsborough *Wicked Lady* costume dramas of the 1940s. Michael Redgrave, on the other hand, was a screen novice, his only previous film appearance being a cameo in Hitchcock's *Secret Agent* two years before. Redgrave brought with him some of the English stage actor's snobbery about filmmaking, but was sufficiently impressed by Hitchcock's control of the medium to turn in a rattling good performance. In his autobiography, Redgrave recalls that films 'were frowned upon by many "serious" artists in the theatre in those days and it should be remembered that, with a few memorable exceptions, British films before 1939 were regarded as something of a laughing stock in England and were almost unknown abroad. Among the exceptions, of course, were the films of Asquith and Hitchcock. . . . From Hitchcock I learned to do as I was told and not to worry too much!'

The Lady Vanishes has Margaret Lockwood as a young English girl on her way back from the Balkans to be married in England. She is befriended on the way by a scatty old English lady Miss Froy (Dame May Whitty) whose disappearance provides the film with its title. The other pas-

sengers deny all knowledge of her; and Radford and Wayne are gloriously dismissive, their only real concern being to get back to England before the end of the Test Match. Only Michael Redgrave's character – albeit grudgingly, and despite thinking her 'a bit of a stinker' – will listen to Miss Lockwood. Together they find Miss Froy and help her to escape back to London, with her top-secret message, while they and the train's other English passengers hold off the sinister agents of a mysterious foreign power. It is flimsy, of course, but a great film nevertheless.

What makes the film so delightful and sustains its delight down the years is the interplay between the characters. Lockwood is intensely convincing as the girl, adamant that she has not imagined the vanishing lady. Hitchcock was fond of this basic plot, and used it as the basis of one of his *Alfred Hitchcock Presents* television shows. Michael Redgrave is whimsical as the flippant but reliable music student; Cecil Parker is convincingly oily as the well-connected adulterer; Dame May Whitty is delightful as the apparently dotty Miss Froy; and Paul Lukas is correctly sinister. But the film belongs to Radford and Wayne as the cricket-mad Charters and Caldicott. Beetle-browed at the beginning, they are desperate to get back to their beloved England because it is on the brink of war, one assumes. Only gradually do we learn that it is only a cricket match which obsesses them.

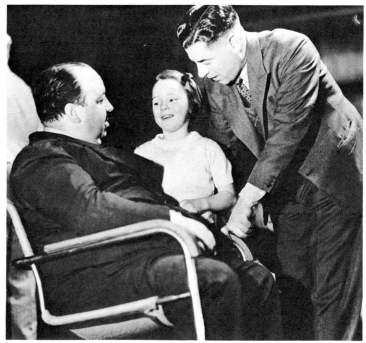

Top: *Michael Regrave and Margaret Lockwood in* The Lady Vanishes.
Above: *Hitchcock and his only daughter Patricia on the set of the* The Lady Vanishes.

Above: *Dame May Whitty (left), the vanishing lady of* The Lady Vanishes.
Opposite: *The immortal Charters and Caldicott in action.*

Charters and Caldicott are the quintessential types who inhabit Noel Coward's *Mad Dogs and Englishmen*. They are impeccably, imperiously English: they dress for dinner at an out of the way mid-European inn; stiffly correct, they miss a vital train because they mistake *Hungarian Rhapsody* for the National Anthem. Later on, interrupting someone else's phone call to England, Radford blusters 'But you *can't* be in England and not know the Test score!' Initially querulous about Miss Lockwood's tale, they deny the existence of Miss Froy as they fear a delay, but are later wholly committed to finding her and ensuring that the sinister foreigners do not dictate what they, English gentlemen, can do. In the otherwise lamentable 1978 remake, with Elliott Gould and Cybill Shepherd no match for Redgrave and Lockwood, only Ian Carmichael and the late Arthur Lowe, playing Charters and Caldicott, emerge with any credibility. The pair were even dusted down for a BBC TV series in 1984, which had Robin Bailey and Michael Aldridge striving to come to terms with London in the 1980s, memorably trying to order a proper pot of tea in a fast-food outlet. Even Launder and Gilliat retained such affection for the couple that they used them twice more, in *Millions like Us* (1943) and in the excellent reworking of *The Lady Vanishes, Night Train to Munich* (1940). In this film Charters buys a copy of *Mein Kampf*. He informs Caldicott that all young German married couples are presented with a copy on their wedding night, to be greeted with the retort

'Oh, I don't think it's that kind of book old man!'

Hitchcock was delighted with the finished screenplay and cast of *The Lady Vanishes*, and he revelled in the MacGuffins in the plot, like the Foreign Office using an elderly English nanny like Dame May as their messenger, and that her 'message' was nothing more than a few bars of a song! It is the audience who naturally assume that those few bars are worth killing for! While some of the film's special effects seem laughable now (the obvious models of the train, the back projection) Hitchcock manages to infuse the narrative with an urgency and drive that he has rarely matched. Margaret Lockwood is utterly convincing as Iris, desperately trying to hang on to her sanity, and when she spots Miss Froy's name written in steam on the window of the restaurant car the audience can be heard *willing* Michael Redgrave to see it too – but by the time he has turned round, it has gone.

The Lady Vanishes was polished off in a fast five-week shoot at the Islington studios in the summer of 1937. Considering the timing of the film, it requires little effort to see the villains as Nazis, battling against British pluck and getting thoroughly trounced for their efforts. Despite all the sinister events, the panacea is always a good strong cup of tea! The true scale of the threat posed by Nazi Germany was still not wholly appreciated; and the beguiling way in which the combined might of Redgrave, Radford and Wayne thrashed the comic-book villains in *The Lady Vanishes* stands as a requiem to that blithe innocence which surrounded the days of appeasement leading up to World War II.

By the time of the film's release Hitchcock was, quite simply, Britain's best-known director. In its review of *The Lady Vanishes*, the *New York Times* called Hitchcock 'England's greatest director . . . when your sides are not aching with laughter, your brain is throbbing in its attempts to outguess the director.' The hand of Hollywood – so long on the horizon – finally reached across the Atlantic and coerced him to Hollywood. Hitchcock had been receiving overtures from the film mogul David O Selznick (he had been friendly with his brother Myron Selznick in London in the 1920s), and was now committed to go to Hollywood to undertake a film about the sinking of the *Titanic*, which sadly was never made. One can only speculate how Hitchcock's version of the sinking of the most famous liner the world has ever known would have fared. Roy Baker's film about the *Titanic, A Night to Remember* (1958), was a workmanlike effort, with the actual sinking spectacularly handled, but one longed for some Hitchcockian vignettes to elevate the subject. It is known that Hitchcock planned to open his film with a shot of one rivet being put in place, then slowly pulling back to reveal the massive bulk of the ship.

Before finally leaving for America, Hitchcock had rashly agreed to film Daphne du Maurier's successful novel *Jamaica Inn*. Hitchcock had been friendly with the novelist's father, the eminent actor Gerald du Maurier, and though claiming no real affection for her work went on to film three du Maurier novels. Charles Laughton was already cast as the star and indeed he and Hitchcock had much in common; they were exactly the same age, large men, who came from comfortable, middle-class Catholic backgrounds (Laughton was born in Scarborough). Laughton was an insular and insecure man; although married to Elsa Lanchester, he was tormented by his double life as a homosexual, which he found difficult to reconcile with his religion. His biographer Charles Higham tells of how after a juvenile misdemeanor, Laughton was chillingly cautioned by a Jesuit father, 'If you do this, my boy, you will be punished through all eternity . . . Do you know what eternity is? It is as if the world were a steel globe, and every thousand years a bird's wing brushed past the globe. The time it would take for that globe to wear away would be all eternity!' Precisely the sort of sentiment to send a chill through Hitchcock's veins. Hitchcock and Laughton had known each other since the late 1920s and used to dine regularly together at L'Etoile. Laughton had formed Mayflower Productions to instigate and develop screen properties with his partner Erich Pommer. Formerly head of the UFA Studios in Berlin, Pommer left on Hitler's accession to power. Laughton and Pommer had snapped up the film rights to the du Maurier novel, which had been an immediate success when it was published in 1936.

Jamaica Inn is a rattling good yarn about a young girl forced to stay in Cornwall with her wicked uncle, the landlord of the infamous Jamaica Inn, a hotbed of smuggling since the 16th century. Writing of Cornwall, Alan Coren brilliantly conjures up the atmosphere of Jamaica Inn: 'Cornwall, where it is always 1790 and rotten weather, the sea pounding the rocks and the wind pounding the trees and all the inhabitants pounding doors in the small hours; Cornwall, where not a vital remains unstapped, or a tush unpished!'

In many ways *Jamaica Inn* prefaces Miss du Maurier's most famous novel *Rebecca*, which was published in 1938 and was to be Hitchcock's next film. Both stories deal with young girls alone in the world and cast adrift in unfamiliar and hostile environments. Hitchcock swiftly realized that *Jamaica*

CHARLES LAUGHTON

IN

JAMAICA INN

Inn 'was an absurd thing to undertake.' Setting up the production was fraught. Hitchcock read the prepared screenplay and disliked it intensely. He was keen to get out of the film if at all possible, even willing to sell his house to pay back his advance if necessary. Laughton however was committed and when Hitchcock told him he felt unable to proceed, Laughton said: 'If you don't, it will ruin Erich. You'll be putting a German refugee on the streets!' Under such moral blackmail Hitchcock proceeded, albeit reluctantly, with the film.

The screenplay was rewritten by Sidney Gilliat, who had impressed Hitchcock with his treatment of *The Lady Vanishes* the previous year, and at Laughton's request J B Priestley was also brought in to build up his part. Hitchcock felt that the novel's one redeeming feature was that it was a whodunnit. The landlord of Jamaica Inn was obviously only a henchman, and the head of the smugglers was a man of substance (the local squire). However, with Laughton cast as Squire Pengallan and also co-producer of the film, he could not be expected to appear only in a cameo at the end of the film. From Hitchcock's point of view therefore the premise of the whole film was undermined from the start and he tackled the subject lackadaisically.

For all its faults, *Jamaica Inn* (1939) enjoyed a stellar cast. Laughton is magnificently hammy as the Squire, but his final line as he plunges from the mast of a ship to avoid capture is 'Tell everyone how the Great Age ended!' which lends a dignity and nobility to an otherwise implausible character. Also notable were Leslie Banks (as Joss the landlord of the inn), Basil Radford, Mervyn Johns, Emlyn Williams and Robert Newton. The film gave Maureen O'Hara her first major film role, but Hitchcock's relationship with her was distant; as usual he was more interested in the mechanics of filmmaking than nurturing the performances of individual actors. Hitchcock seemed to take an almost sadistic delight in his power as director. For one scene O'Hara was required to stand and be buffeted by tides and lashed by rain, a physically demanding scene which easily could have been tackled by a stand-in, but Hitchcock insisted that she endure the discomfort herself. Laughton, however, grew very fond of O'Hara, even at one point wishing to adopt her!

On release *Jamaica Inn* was a considerable box-office success, which enhanced Hitchcock's reputation, but it was one of the most vexing films he ever directed and made him all the more keen to make the move to America. Graham Greene was particularly scathing about the film, criticizing the 'frequent failures in imagination . . . no surprises and no suspense . . . I was irresistibly reminded of an all star charity matinee.' It was unfortunate that Hitchcock's British period was to end on such a low note. Immediately on completion Laughton and Pommer's Mayflower Productions ceased business; Laughton and Maureen O'Hara left for Hollywood to start work on *The Hunchback of Notre Dame*; and Mr and Mrs Alfred Hitchcock and their daughter Patricia, then aged 11, set sail for the United States where he would launch the second half of his career with the filming of another Daphne du Maurier novel – *Rebecca*.

Right: *Hitchcock in a break during filming.*
Opposite: *Poster for* Jamaica Inn *(1939), the last film he made before leaving for Hollywood.*

VINTAGE HOLLYWOOD

The Hollywood which greeted Alfred Hitchcock in March 1939 was the undisputed film capital of the world. Hitchcock had made brief private visits to the United States in 1937 and 1938, but had waited until now before working there. Hollywood was more than half the world away from Europe. Europe was preparing for war, few had any doubts about that; while Chamberlain was being deluded by the chicanery of the Nazis, the military machine of the Third Reich was readying itself for war. America, however, remained blithely unconcerned with European squabbles; the isolationist policy was in full swing, and Hollywood was geared as efficiently as the Reich but in a wholly different direction. It was at the height of its success as the purveyor of dreams which, for so many around the world, film had come to delineate. In 1939 alone such classics as *Gone with the Wind, Stagecoach, Of Mice and Men, Goodbye Mr Chips, Ninotchka, Wuthering Heights, Mr Smith goes to Washington* and *The Wizard of Oz* were released. Stars such as Clark Gable, Greta Garbo, James Stewart, Bette Davis and Henry Fonda were at their peak.

The American Dream Factory was also home to a flourishing expatriate British community, stars who had come to represent the very essence of 'Englishness' in the eyes of the world, like Ronald Colman, David Niven, C Aubrey Smith, Basil Rathbone and Nigel Bruce. The British invasion had begun early in the history of Hollywood, with peripatetic players such as Charlie Chaplin and Stan Laurel drifting into the embryonic film capital. The center of the expatriate community was the delightfully incongruous Hollywood Cricket Club, where you could see such unlikely scenes as Errol Flynn batting and Boris Karloff keeping wicket.

Laurence Olivier and Vivien Leigh were the brightest stars in Hollywood at that time. Leigh had landed the role of a lifetime playing Scarlett O'Hara in Selznick's lavish production of *Gone with the Wind*, while Olivier, after an initial mistrust of the cinema, had won rave reviews for his portrayal of Heathcliff in William Wyler's film of *Wuthering Heights*.

Previous pages: *Robert Benchley and Joel McCrea in* Foreign Correspondent *(1940)*.
Left: *Portrait of Hitchcock soon after his arrival in Hollywood.*
Below: *Alma in Hollywood.*

Other notable Brits included such stalwarts as Roland Young and the laconic George Sanders, who wrote: 'I am not one of those people who would rather act than eat; quite the reverse. Larry Olivier was born with the desire to act. I was not. My own desire as a boy was to retire! That ambition has never changed!' Sanders revelled in the glorious hedonism of Hollywood, others were not so happy. Cedric Hardwicke wrote in 1935: 'God felt sorry for actors, so he gave them a place in the sun and a swimming pool; all they had to sacrifice was their talent.' Alfred and Alma Hitchcock were never particularly enamored of the 'Hollywood English,' preferring to keep their distance from the clique, although they preserved a particular brand of insular Englishness in their private life. Other stars who kept their distance included Leslie Howard, Robert Donat, Laurence Olivier and Vivien Leigh – they simply came to film there, disliked the place intensely, and were only too keen to get on the next plane out. On his arrival in Hollywood Olivier was shaken to find a curt note from C Aubrey Smith, the doyen of the English community, saying 'There will be nets practice tomorrow at 4pm. I trust I shall see you there!'

Selznick was a mogul on the grand scale; he was responsible for such elegant vehicles as the 1937 production of *A Star Is Born* (1937) and *The Prisoner of Zenda* (1937). He lived and breathed film, and spent years working toward the apogee of his career, *Gone with the Wind*, which was released to worldwide acclaim in 1939. Obviously something special was required to follow *Gone with the Wind*, and Selznick was delighted when he purchased the screen rights to *Rebecca*, which had been published in 1938 and was, after Margaret Mitchell's *Gone with the Wind*, the most popular novel of the decade. Hitchcock had himself been keen to purchase the film rights while he was filming *The Lady Vanishes* but baulked at the asking price.

The prepublicity surrounding *Gone with the Wind* was extraordinary even by Hollywood's excessive standards. As soon as it was announced that Selznick had acquired the screen rights to the epic Civil War novel, it seemed as though everyone in America was talking about his plans. These days, the hype is best remembered for the mystery and controversy surrounding the casting of Scarlett O'Hara; virtually every

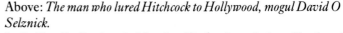

Above: *The man who lured Hitchcock to Hollywood, mogul David O Selznick.*
Left: *Novelist Daphne du Maurier. Hitchcock made three films based on her work, including his last in Britian and his first in Hollywood.*

major actress in Hollywood was tested and talent scouts scoured the country before the role finally went to Vivien Leigh.

Overjoyed at the attendant publicity, Selznick launched a scaled-down search to play the unnamed heroine in *Rebecca* (cunningly, Daphne du Maurier never named her throughout the novel's 375 pages, a device which Hitchcock retained in the film; thankfully Selznick rejected Hitchcock's idea of calling her 'Daphne'). Among those seriously considered for the coveted role were Loretta Young and Margaret Sullavan, although from an early stage Selznick was convinced of Joan Fontaine's suitability for the role. Selznick's decision surprised a lot of his Hollywood associates. Fontaine was known as 'the wooden woman' and her long-running feud with her sister, Olivia de Havilland, was probably better known than her acting abilities. Like the Hitchcocks, Fontaine kept herself isolated from the Hollywood English whom she considered 'a cliquey lot who would sit in each other's dressing rooms, swapping theatre stories and recalling old chums from their Mayfair days.' Ironically, the cast of *Rebecca* was a virtual who's who of that same crowd.

A strong contender for the role, certainly from the leading man's point of view, was Vivien Leigh, whose well-publicized affair with Laurence Olivier was reaching its height. Olivier was pitching desperately for Leigh; this contributed, perhaps, to his antipathy to Fontaine during filming. Neither Selznick nor Hitchcock were at all keen on the idea, for while respecting Vivien's abilities as an actress, it was obvious to both that she was far too attractive and seductive to play the role of the mousy heroine. Had the eponymous character ever appeared in the film, Vivien Leigh would have been ideal for the role of Rebecca, the woman that the character Frank Crawley described as 'the most beautiful creature I ever saw in my life!' Laurence Olivier was already cast as Max, although there had been strong competition; Hitchcock favored Robert Donat and both Leslie Howard and William Powell were keen to have the role. Many people felt that Ronald Colman would have been ideal casting, but the urbane Colman declined on the grounds that he did not cherish the idea of playing a wife murderer!

Daphne du Maurier's novel was a massive success; in Britain it was reprinted an astonishing seven times during its first year of publication. Millions of people took it to heart, identifying strongly with the predicament of the nameless heroine, forever overshadowed by the omniscient and ghostly presence of the dead Rebecca. Together with the odium of Mrs Danvers and the demands of Manderley, this leads to a growing alienation between Maxim and his new wife. Orson Welles had produced and starred in a radio version of *Rebecca* in December 1938 which had been a massive success and whetted people's appetites for the film.

Selznick was keen to keep as strictly to the novel as possible, seeing in its existing fans a readymade audience of millions. Prior to his arrival in Hollywood, Hitchcock had commissioned Joan Harrison (the only member of his English team he took with him to work in America) and Philip MacDonald to work on the screenplay, but Selznick's reaction to their treatment did not bode well. Selznick wrote to Hitchcock that he was 'shocked and disappointed' by the treatment. Hitchcock, he claimed, had 'removed all the subtleties and substituted big, broad strokes which in outline form betray just how ordinary the actual plot is and just how bad a picture it would make.' Selznick found Hitchcock's early scenes of seasickness 'cheap beyond words' and damningly wrote: 'The first portrait of Max smoking a cigar that makes other passengers ill is not my idea of an introduction for a romantic and mysterious figure.' Reading Selznick's voluminous correspondence on this matter, one realizes just how large a part he played in making it such a successful and timeless adaptation. Mercifully, however, Hitchcock fought against one sensational Selznick ploy, that the smoke from the burning Manderley would form into a letter 'R'! Selznick called in the distinguished dramatist Robert Sherwood to lend the script a certain luster, the touch which Sherwood had lent to films such as *The Petrified Forest* and *Waterloo Bridge* prior to *Rebecca*.

Below: *Laurence Olivier and Joan Fontaine in the boathouse scene from* Rebecca *(1940).*

Top: *Production drawing for opening scene of* Rebecca, *showing derelict Manderley.*
Above: *Publicity shot from* Rebecca *with Hitchcock eyeing George Sanders.*
Opposite: *The unnamed heroine (Joan Fontaine) and the evil Mrs Danvers (Judith Anderson).*

Hitchcock was too astute not to see the popular appeal of the novel, but personally he found it 'an old-fashioned novelette lacking in humour.' He did, however, keep a number of du Maurier's incidents, such as the odious Mrs Van Hopper stubbing out her cigarette in a jar of face cream (a touch he later reused in *To Catch a Thief*). Filming began in July 1939 with an all-star cast which stands as the definitive roll call of the Hollywood British: aside from Fontaine and Olivier, Gladys Cooper, Nigel Bruce, George Sanders, Reginald Denny, C Aubrey Smith and Leo G Carroll could be glimpsed amid the Manderley shrubbery. Hitchcock's first American film, *Rebecca* is more English than beer and skittles.

From the opening shot of the deserted, mist-swathed mansion of Manderley, through to its fiery conclusion, *Rebecca* is a classic example of cinematic storytelling, revelling in its atmosphere and with stalwart playing from all concerned. Hitchcock saw it as a fairy tale, and the essential romance of the novel was not lost in its transition to the screen.

'Last night I dreamt I went to Manderley again . . .' is the most poignant opening line in cinema, plunging the audience into over two hours of narrative cinema at its best. The audience knows that the house is a model, that Olivier and Fontaine are not really on the Riviera, that the Cornish cliffs are Californian and that the new Mrs de Winter would complain more vehemently about the sinister presence of Mrs Danvers, but the audience is swept along and only afterward do niggling doubts occur. Even these are promptly dismissed as the film is seen again and we all walk down the deserted drive to Manderley.

Rebecca is Hitchcock at his masterly best. While he had his reservations about the film, it nevertheless stands as a supreme example of his craft. What makes it so endearing is its timeless quality; one cannot imagine an England such as this yet, along with *Mrs Miniver, Rebecca* stands as a supreme example of Englishness not as it really was, but as it ought to have been.

The ensemble playing is unmatched. Joan Fontaine is perfect as the mousy heroine – Hitchcock encouraged the rest of the cast to keep their distance from her on set to ensure she felt the isolation of her character. Olivier is compelling as the haunted Max, perfectly matching du Maurier's description: 'His face was arresting, sensitive, medieval in some strange inexplicable way, and I was reminded of . . . a past where men walked cloaked at night, and stood in the shadows of old doorways, a past of narrow stairways and dim dungeons, a past of whispers in the dark, of shimmering rapier blades, of silent, exquisite courtesy.' George Sanders is suavely sinister as Rebecca's cousin Favell, Reginald Denny fine and upstanding as Frank Crawley, and Gladys Cooper and Nigel Bruce impeccable as Max's sister- and brother-in-law. Judith Anderson, in only her second film, is ominous as the ubiquitous Mrs Danvers. (Hitchcock had been keen to cast Flora Robson as Mrs Danvers, but she had just finished playing the housekeeper in *Wuthering Heights* and declined the opportunity.)

In *Rebecca* a gauche young girl meets the suave and mysterious Maxim de Winter holidaying on the French Riviera. He is there to try to forget the death of his first wife, the beautiful Rebecca. He is captivated by the innocent young girl, and asks her if she would wish to accompany him to the family home Manderley, in Cornwall. 'Do you need a secretary or something?' she naively replies. 'I'm asking you to marry me, you little fool' rejoins Maxim, in one of the screen's less romantic proposals. Once back at Manderley, the new Mrs de Winter is terrified of the housekeeper Mrs Danvers, who adored Rebecca. It is revealed that Maxim, far from adoring Rebecca, despised her for her philandering and promiscuity, and it looks as though he will have to stand trial for her murder. Maxim is blackmailed by her cousin Favell but a last-minute visit to a doctor in London reveals that Rebecca was dying of cancer and so her suicide was highly likely. Returning home by car, Frank Crawley points out the Northern Lights to Maxim who snaps back, 'That's not the Northern Lights, That's Manderley!' On arriving at the blazing mansion, Maxim is overjoyed to find his new wife has escaped from the inferno, while the evil Mrs Danvers can be seen perishing in the fire which she started to avenge Rebecca's memory.

Above: *Joan Fontaine dressed for the Manderley fancy dress ball.*

Hitchcock's *Rebecca* is the definitive three-handkerchief romance. Hitchcock was well aware of the story's fairy-tale elements, confirmed by an early line of Favell to Mrs Danvers, 'Careful, Danny, we don't want to shock Cinderella, do we?' From her first appearance Mrs Danvers is clearly one of the ugly sisters. Cleverly, Hitchcock rarely allowed Judith Anderson to be seen moving; he lets her materialize in scenes so that we see the story through the girl's eyes, with Mrs Danvers suddenly appearing like an ever-present threat. The film is full of other domineering women: the snobbish and vulgar Mrs Van Hopper, the horsy Beatrice Lacey, the demonic Mrs Danvers and above all the dead Rebecca, whose presence overshadows the whole film. Manderley comes across as a kind of Hollywood Gormenghast with Joan

Fontaine flitting through it. Rarely better than as the gauche bride, completely at a loss in this vast house, at one point she answers the phone in her morning room with 'Mrs de Winter? I'm sorry, she died some time ago!'

Despite the length, there is an economy in the film. There is a very effective compressed narrative at the beginning; the shot shows Olivier at the cliff's edge which conveys his deep unhappiness at Rebecca's death. The audience assumes his next move will be suicide. Olivier excels in his part. His personal frustration at not playing opposite Vivien Leigh lends just the right degree of remoteness to his scenes with Joan Fontaine. George Sanders is also superb, his smooth voice comes into its own in the blackmailing scene in the back of Max's Rolls-Royce. In the revelatory boathouse scene Fontaine finds Olivier sitting like little boy lost after learning that Rebecca's body has been discovered. Without resorting to flashback, under Hitchcock's tutelage Olivier spellbindingly tells his new wife the true story of his marriage to Rebecca.

Rebecca is an uncharacteristic Hitchcock film. The actual suspense is muted and what gives the film its durable impact is that Hitchcock tells a love story – a proper love story, developing it through courtship, to marriage, disillusion and sadness, with flesh and blood characters not mere ciphers.

The budget for *Rebecca* was $1 million and Selznick bombarded Hitchcock with memos about the length of time he was taking to shoot the film: 'My fondness for you personally, and my respect for your abilities, cannot blind me to my responsibility to the people who are financing these pictures, and to the employees whose jobs depend on efficient shooting on the stage . . .' Selznick was like a mother hen during shooting, inundating Hitchcock with his infamous memos (years later, Hitchcock said he was thinking of filming one of Selznick's memos as 'The Longest Story Ever Told'). Selznick was particularly worried that the wholly English cast might be too cultured for the folks in Middle America and felt that the cast should phrase their dialogue so as 'to avoid anything which might be difficult for an American audience to understand.' One particular memo must have caused Hitchcock to raise a wry eyebrow and wonder whether his move to Hollywood was such a good idea. Selznick wrote: 'From this point on to the end, I'd like to urge that you be a little more Yiddish Art Theater . . . a little less English Repertory Theater.'

Overriding even Selznick's monumental problems during the shooting of *Rebecca* was the threat of war in Europe. On its outbreak in September 1939, Selznick and Hitchcock were concerned about the eligibility of stars such as Laurence Olivier and George Sanders for wartime service. Olivier particularly was champing at the bit to return to England to do his bit. Hitchcock was obviously unsuitable for war service, he was 40 years old, overweight and had a family; but in the climate of hysterical jingoism which characterized the Phony War of late 1939 and early 1940, no one was exempt from doing their bit for King and Country.

In many ways *Rebecca* is an ideal film for Hitchcock's Hollywood debut. It stands as a poignant epitaph for all that England was in the process of losing. The empty house ablaze is a salutary warning of the Blitz to come. The opening scene with its wistfulness for that which has been lingers, while the cool narration of Joan Fontaine takes us back to the long-lost dreams, the disillusion and madness which lie on the road to Manderley . . .

In August 1940, after the German Blitzkrieg across Belgium and France, when Britain stood alone facing the Nazi armies massed across the Channel, Michael Balcon wrote an acerbic piece in an English paper: 'I had a plump young junior technician in my studios whom I promoted from department to department. Today he is one of our most famous directors and he is in Hollywood, while we are left behind shorthanded, trying to harness the films to our great national effort.'

Stung by the accusations, Hitchcock replied that the British government 'has only to call upon me for my services. The manner in which I am helping my country is not Mr Balcon's business, and has nothing to do with patriotic ideals.' The British expatriate community in Hollywood were popularly known in Britain as those who had 'Gone with the Wind-Up.' However His Majesty's Government gave encouragement through their Consulate in Los Angeles and admitted that British actors and technicians were far better employed in Hollywood, helping make films which conveyed an image of England which made it worth fighting for. Churchill himself strongly believed in the power of cinema propaganda, feeling that it helped to stress the bonds between Britain and the United States, helping to isolate the isolationists and encourage America into the war. He singled out such films as *Lady Hamilton* (with Olivier and Leigh) and *Mrs Miniver* as having a considerable impact on the war effort.

Below: *The tense windmill scene in* Foreign Correspondent. *Joel McCrea plays a newspaperman who becomes involved in intrigue when Nazis capture a Dutch diplomat.*

Hitchcock's next film, *Foreign Correspondent*(1940), was a valuable contribution to the war effort. Despite being less than happy with the casting of Joel McCrea and Laraine Day as the central characters (Hitchcock had wanted Gary Cooper) he persevered with the film. Hitchcock's old collaborators Charles Bennett and Joan Harrison worked with the director fashioning a screenplay from the autobiography *Personal History* by Vincent Sheean. Additional dialogue was by the eminent authors James Hilton and Robert Benchley, who also had a cameo role as Stebbins in the finished film.

The plot of *Foreign Correspondent* concerns an American newspaperman (McCrea) in Europe on the eve of World War II who finds himself more involved than he wished. McCrea is increasingly drawn into the intrigue when he meets an elderly Dutch diplomat who is kidnapped by the Nazis. In true Hitchcock style McCrea gives chase, and in the process falls in love. The object of his affections, played by Laraine Day, is the daughter of an Englishman posing as the aristocratic head of a pacifist organization who turns out to be a Nazi spy. At the end of their adventure McCrea and Day return to America, only to find that her father is trying to escape on the same plane. When the plane is shot down by the Nazis, the father sacrifices his life for his daughter.

A number of set-pieces in the film are remarkable. Hitchcock had a field day with the 'Dutch' locations – as with *The Secret Agent* and its Swiss themes, Hitchcock thought what Holland was famous for and came up with tulips and windmills. There is a nail-biting chase scene in an old windmill to which the kidnapped diplomat is taken, and a chase across the

flat lands of Holland. In this scene McCrea is aided and abetted by a reporter called ffolliott (played by the suave George Sanders) who while being shot at by Nazi agents still finds time to ramble on at inordinate length about the spelling of the family name. The murder in the rainstorm near the beginning of the film is a Hitchcock landmark: before a sea of faceless umbrellas, a murder is committed and the murderer escapes, a bravura scene from Hitchcock. The villains also attempt to murder McCrea from the top of the Catholic Westminster Cathedral which over 40 years later was to be the scene of Alfred Hitchcock's memorial service. Technically the most assured moment is the plane crash at the end of the film. Hitchcock had a transparent screen built into the front of an enormous tank of water which gave the impression of the plane diving toward the sea. On impact it bursts, and the 'sea' floods the cockpit. Hitchcock proudly told Truffaut that the shot was achieved in one take without a single cut.

Stung by criticism of his 'unpatriotism' Hitchcock gave Joel McCrea the following speech to deliver at the conclusion of *Foreign Correspondent*: 'Hello America, I've been watching part of the world being blown to pieces. A part of the world as nice as Vermont, Ohio, Virginia, California and Illinois lies ripped up, bleeding like a steer in a slaughterhouse. And I've seen things that make the history of the savages read like the Pollyanna legend! . . . All that noise you hear isn't static it's

death coming to London . . . It's too late now to do anything except stand in the dark and let them come, as if the lights are out everywhere except in America . . . Hang on to your lights, they're the only lights in the world!' It is a powerful piece of propaganda, given America's isolationist stance at the time, but it is to Hitchcock's credit that it sits easily in the context of the film as a whole. Sheridan Morley astutely observed that with 'those few words, it is arguable that Hitchcock did more for the "war effort" than his detractors back home were ever to achieve in the same cause!' *Foreign Correspondent* was also praised by one who knew more than his fair share about propaganda. Josef Goebbels called it a 'Masterpiece of propaganda, a first-class production which no doubt will make a certain impression . . . in enemy countries.'

Hitchcock followed *Foreign Correspondent* with a trip to war-torn London to resettle his mother and brother into his own country house. On his return to Los Angeles Hitchcock was keen to film George Bernard Shaw's play *The Devil's Disciple*. However, Shaw refused to release the film rights at this time as he felt that a film showing America and Britain at war would be detrimental to Britain's war effort, and the play was not filmed until 1959. Hitchcock's next film, *Mr and Mrs Smith* (1941), was made purely as a concession to his friend Carole Lombard, who was at that time married to Clark Gable. The couple were indisputably the king and queen of

Left: *The brilliantly constructed assassination which sets the scene for* Foreign Correspondent *(1940).*
Above: *Hitchcock's favorite prop from* Foreign Correspondent, *the mobile plane wing.*
Below: *The ebullient Carole Lombard from the comedy* Mr & Mrs Smith *(1941).*

Hollywood and a Lombard picture would certainly do no harm at all to Hitchcock's reputation. Tragically it proved to be Lombard's penultimate film as she died the following year in a plane crash while on a War Bonds promotion tour. The film was based on an original screenplay by American playwright Norman Krasna, who had written such successful romantic films as *Bachelor Mother* and *The Flame of New Orleans*. *Mr and Mrs Smith* was as light as fluff. A divorced couple (played by Lombard and Robert Montgomery) gradually come to realize the strength of their love and eventually come back together again. Hitchcock admitted: 'I really didn't understand the type of people who were portrayed in the film, all I did was photograph the scenes as written.' The making of the film, however, was good fun, with Hitchcock and Lombard striking up an excellent relationship. Arriving for the first day of shooting Hitchcock found that Miss Lombard had constructed a corral containing three cows bearing the names of the film's stars on placards around their necks – taking Hitchcock's oft-quoted remark that 'actors are cattle' literally! Miss Lombard also insisted on directing Hitch's cameo appearance and relished her power and the incongruity of the situation. She made the director undergo take after take before pronouncing herself satisfied. *Mr and Mrs Smith* was a lightweight diversion for Hitchcock and the film stands as an agreeable 'screwball' comedy.

Above: *The Hitchcock family relaxing in the early 1940s.*
Below: *Joan Fontaine's first meeting with ne'er-do-well Cary Grant, whom she later marries in* Suspicion *(1941).*

With his third American film completed within two years of his arrival, Hitchcock had established himself in Hollywood, on his own terms. He and Alma and their daughter Patricia remained a self-contained family who mingled little with the English community or indeed the established Hollywood film people. But just as he did not succumb to the Hollywood English and never really became an American (despite taking US citizenship in 1955) neither was Hitchcock ever a middle-class fruiterer's son. He simply *was* Alfred Hitchcock, as much an invention as any of his film characters. He always turned up on set in an immaculate suit and tie, however blistering the location, and took *The Times* of London to the end of his life. Hitchcock cultivated a certain image of himself assiduously, particularly enjoying his reputation as a gourmet and connoisseur of fine wines.

In the same way that Hitchcock's films created their own worlds, despite the locale or studio setting, Alma and Alfred together created their own world in the heart of Los Angeles. With England at war, and the antipathy aroused by Balcon's condemnation of him, Hitchcock was more isolated than ever. As was his wont Hitchcock's response was to immerse himself in making films. Alma, his ever-devoted wife and collaborator, had begun work with the faithful Joan Harrison on an adaptation of Francis Iles' novel, *Before the Fact*, which

was to become *Suspicion*. Some additional dialogue was to be supplied later by Samson Raphaelson, a Hollywood immortal who had written the play which was the basis for the world's first talking picture *The Jazz Singer* and who had also collaborated fruitfully with Ernst Lubitsch. However Hitchcock was not altogether happy with the finished script, was in danger of losing his favorite cameraman, and both he and Joan Fontaine were ill during the filming, but like true professionals they adhered to the old showbiz motto that 'the show must go on.'

Suspicion (1941) was Hitchcock's first experience of working with Cary Grant, who by 1941 was established as one of Hollywood's leading stars with such distinguished films as *Bringing up Baby, His Girl Friday* and *The Philadelphia Story* to his credit. Both men were enthusiastic about working together, although Grant was also less than happy with the finished screenplay because it showed him as a wife murderer (the same reservation which Ronald Colman had about *Rebecca*). Hitchcock revealed: 'The real ending I had for the film was that Grant brings his wife the fatal glass of milk to kill her. She knows she is going to be killed so she writes a letter to her mother saying "I'm in love with him, I don't want to live anymore, he's going to kill me, society should be protected." Folding up the letter she leaves it by the bed and says to him "Would you mind mailing it for me?" She drinks the milk, he watches her die. The last shot of the picture, Cary Grant whistling very cheerfully, goes to the mailbox and pops in the letter . . . But it was heresy to do that to Cary Grant in those days!' As a compromise between Hitchcock and the studio, it was suggested that Grant is seen murdering his wife, but in the time-honored Hollywood tradition is dispatched to the RAF and war to atone for his sins, where he becomes a hero and is killed in glorious battle.

The RKO Studio was plainly unhappy with Hitchcock's intention and after he had completed the shooting they ruthlessly cut the footage down in his absence to under an hour, expunging all possibility of Cary Grant being a wife murderer. However even the studio realized that the resulting film was untenable, and Hitchcock was allowed to restore some dignity (and length) to the film. Hitchcock was plainly unhappy with the ending, which diffused all the dark side of his craft. The finished film is accurately titled, for in the final cut it is only Joan Fontaine's *suspicion* that her husband is trying to kill her, and at the end of the film they are seen driving off happily together. Hitchcock was not alone in his distaste for the ending. *The Hollywood Reporter* in its review commented: 'If this sop of a happy ending was dragged in by the heels, as it appears, it serves only to spoil a great picture.' In fact the controversial ending was not as arbitrary as it seems; RKO previewed the film to the public extensively with both a happy and unhappy ending, and the former was convincingly preferred. Even the film's title posed problems, and a Gallup poll was commissioned to try out a number of titles on the public, including *Fright*, but the public preferred *Suspicion*. Despite this troubled genesis, most critics agreed that the film was a satisfactory successor to *Rebecca* and it went on to become RKO's biggest grossing film of 1941.

There are, indeed, many similarities between *Rebecca* and *Suspicion*: both deal with resigned spinsters (both played by Joan Fontaine) who are unexpectedly liberated from their unhappy circumstances by a charming man who whisks them to an environment worse than that from which they have escaped. In both cases, fortunately, they triumph with a happy

Above: *Cary Grant and Joan Fontaine under Hitchcock's direction while filming* Suspicion.

ending. As well as Joan Fontaine, *Suspicion* also featured a number of familiar faces: Nigel Bruce and Leo G Carroll from *Rebecca*, Dame May Whitty from *The Lady Vanishes* and Isabel Jeans from *Downhill*.

Suspicion is steeped in that rococo Englishness which had made *Rebecca* so attractive – the film is set in a timeless England. In the 1940s there was always some corner of a foreign studio that was forever England, an England where the horse brasses gleam, Dame May Whitty endlessly dispenses tea, Cedric Hardwicke puffs at his pipe behind *The Times* and the church clock stands permanently at ten to three!

Despite the studio's interference over the ending, there are enough flourishes in *Suspicion* to maintain it as a Hitchcock film. The one scene of which Hitchcock was particularly proud is Grant's walk up the staircase at the film's conclusion, bearing his wife a glass of milk which may – or may not – contain poison. To ensure that the audience's eyes are glued to the glass, Hitchcock ingeniously had a light bulb placed in the glass, making it shine with an incandescent glow. There is also a macabre dinner party, with Grant discussing the perfect murder with a neighbor, who conveniently happens to be a thriller writer, and her cadaverous brother, a pathologist who speaks of 'a rather interesting corpse' as he lovingly dissects his poussin.

In *Suspicion*, Hitchcock managed to extract one of Cary Grant's finest performances. The star's biographer Geoffrey Wansell, in his book *Cary Grant: Haunted Idol*, had nothing but praise for Hitchcock's technique: 'What Hitchcock instinctively realized was that Grant's sleek charm disguised a darker and more brooding side of his character, that a chilly, potentially manipulative quality lay behind the comic timing and the dark, heavy handsomeness. He extended the image the audience had become used to by revealing what it might conceal, but he and he alone was permitted by Grant to do so. With other directors he restricted himself to the familiar image of the man in the smiling mask.' It was a transformation which the critics responded to. The *New Yorker* wrote that 'Cary Grant finds a new field for himself, the field of crime, the smiling villain, without heart or conscience. Crime lends color to his amiability.' Grant's Johnny Aysgarth in the film was a charming ne'er-do-well, forever penurious, living on his wits, and sharing an address in The Albany with that Victorian 'gentleman thief' A J Raffles. Joan Fontaine too had matured in the year since *Rebecca*, and her performance in *Suspicion* was poignant and touching, a role for which she justifiably won her only Oscar. She rarely attained the heights she achieved in her work with Hitchcock, although she distinguished herself in *Jane Eyre* and *Letter from an Unknown Woman* before dipping into wholly unmemorable work in the 1950s.

While Hitchcock may have dismissed actors as 'cattle,' in reality he saw his stars as cogs in the elaborate machine of filmmaking, their presence adding to the picture's box-office potential. James Mason recalled that Hitchcock had 'a very clear view of the value of the stars he employed,' remembering Hitchcock telling him that the name of James Stewart on a Hitchcock film could bring in $1 million more, particularly from the Mid-West, than Cary Grant's! It is to his credit that Hitchcock was able to gain such fine performances from his stars – both Cary Grant and James Stewart gave the best performances of their careers in his films. During his half century of filmmaking, Hitchcock extracted great perform-

Above: *Joan Fontaine (left) receiving her Oscar for* Suspicion.
Below: *Robert Cummings (center) becomes involved with Nazis in* Saboteur *(1942).*

Above: *Robert Cummings and Priscilla Lane evading capture in* Saboteur.

ances from such impeccable actors as James Mason, Claude Rains and William Devane, who cherished the opportunity to work with Hitchcock but came to expect little in the way of reciprocation. It was a satisfactory process though; the actors were grateful for the opportunity to work with 'The Master,' appreciating that a credit in a Hitchcock film could enhance their standing. For his part Hitchcock was always happy with actors who arrived on a set word perfect, with no wearisome queries about motivation, happy to accept his direction wholeheartedly.

With *Suspicion* completed, Hitchcock turned to make another contribution to the war effort. By 1942 America had been drawn into the war. Following the unprovoked Japanese attack on Pearl Harbor in December 1941, isolationists were in a welcome minority, and all hands were linked to forge the Atlantic Alliance. Hollywood's major contribution was the lavish, well-intentioned but ultimately unsatisfactory *Forever and a Day* (1942). A sprawling epic which told the story of a London house from 1804 to 1942, it rollcalled every single member of the Hollywood English. Recognizable were numerous members of Hitchcock's repertory company, including C Aubrey Smith, Nigel Bruce, Claude Rains, Charles Laughton and a bewildering 21 scriptwriters and five directors. Hitchcock was meant to have supervised the scene where a cockney housemaid (Ida Lupino) witnesses Queen Victoria's Diamond Jubilee of 1897, but ill health meant he

could not meet his commitment, and René Clair took over the cameo.

Hitchcock's next film *Saboteur* (1942) deals with the topical theme of Nazi saboteurs at work in US aircraft factories. It was Hitchcock's warning to watch out for the enemy within, the Fifth Column. In parts *Saboteur* recalls earlier Hitchcock works such as *The 39 Steps* and *Sabotage* (with which it is often confused because of the similarity of titles). *Saboteur* features Robert Cummings as the central figure; an archetypal Hitchcock hero, he is wrongfully accused of sabotage, and goes on the run pursued by the real saboteurs and police. Recalling *The 39 Steps*, in one scene Cummings unwittingly finds himself in the lair of the saboteurs, and the heroine at first disbelieves Cummings, but then aids him in his escape. However the two central characters were nowhere near as strong or convincing as Robert Donat or Madeleine Carroll. Bob Cummings, an amiable, lightweight American leading man, had appeared with distinction in *Kings Row* the year before. However Hitchcock had severe doubts concerning his suitability for the role, considering him 'a competent performer, but he belongs to the light-comedy class of actors. Aside from that, he has an amusing face, so that even when he's in desperate straits, his features don't convey any anguish.' There was no animosity between director and star though, and Cummings appeared in Hitchcock's *Dial M for Murder* 12 years later. For the female lead Hitchcock was forced to accept Priscilla Lane. She had come to Hollywood as a band singer before switching to acting, and starred in *The Roaring Twenties* (1940).

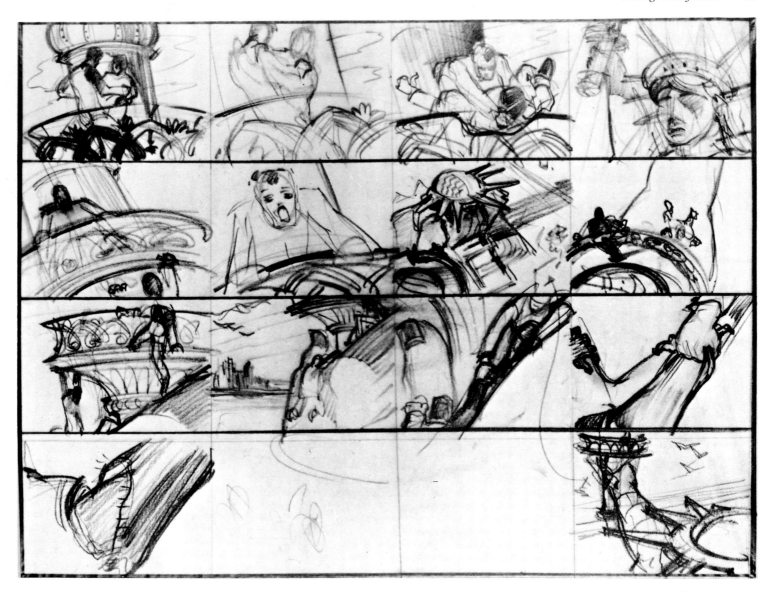

Above: Production sketches for the classic Statue of Liberty scene at the end of Saboteur.

Opposite: Norman Lloyd's life hangs by a thread in Saboteur.

Unusually, the screenplay was based on an original idea by Hitchcock, and he was lucky in gaining the co-operation of the legendary Dorothy Parker. She supplied a number of scenes which Hitchcock enjoyed although he felt they were a little highbrow for the average audience, recalling his oft-quoted view of audiences as 'the moron masses.' Parker's Hollywood work was more successful than that of her contemporary Scott Fitzgerald, but never matched the brilliance of her witty criticism or poetry. One scene both Hitchcock and Parker were pleased with showed Cummings and Lane on the run and taking shelter in a coach full of circus freaks, who are sympathetic, because they too are 'outcasts.' The situation recalls Tod Browning's *Freaks*, which had been made in 1932, but was banned for years because it showed real circus freaks which contemporary audiences found disturbing.

The most famous scene in *Saboteur* is when the real saboteur plunges to his death from the Statue of Liberty. It is typical of Hitchcock to use the Statue – the very symbol of America itself – for the climax of his film. But typically, Hitchcock builds up the suspense to an almost unbearable level, with the saboteur (Norman Lloyd) watching terrified as the shoulder starts splitting from his jacket, leaving his life literally hanging by a thread before plunging to his death. For all the sustained brilliance of the scene, Hitchcock felt it was seriously flawed because if the hero instead of the villain had been hanging in midair 'the audience's anguish would have been greater.'

Another effective scene from *Saboteur* shows the runaway couple trapped in a ballroom of kindly, sympathetic people, like the party from *Young and Innocent*. Cummings and Lane are threatened, fearing for their very lives, but around them are smiling faces quite unaware of their peril. The element of danger is subdued, the villains only hover, but the audience know that if the two central characters approach any one of them, they will be betrayed. This is a masterly example of one of Hitchcock's landmarks: menace is shown in the most seemingly innocuous situations, the heart of danger set amid a sea of smiling faces.

The entire cast and only set of Lifeboat *(1943).*

THE
WAR YEARS

Top: Shadow of a Doubt *(1943). Charlie (Teresa Wright) and her*
Uncle Charlie (Joseph Cotten) converse while her father (Henry Travers)
looks on.
Above: *Charlie survives one of her uncle's murder attempts.*

One of Hitchcock's criticisms of *Saboteur*, his previous film,
was that it was 'cluttered with too many ideas,' its sweep too
wide, as if trying to encompass the scope of America itself.
For his next film, Hitchcock scaled everything down, and
focused on a small town in California, where everyone knew
everyone else, and danger seemed more out of place. It is
exactly this feeling of cosy domesticity, of safe, secure small
town life which makes *Shadow of a Doubt* (1943) so effective,
and why it remained one of Hitchcock's favorite films.

Hitchcock revealed to Ken Ferguson in 1970 that he was
so fond of the film 'because of the combination of character,
suspense and reality. It was one of those rare occasions when
you could combine character with suspense. Usually in a
suspense story there isn't time to develop character.' *Shadow
of a Doubt* concerns Charlie Oakley (Joseph Cotten) who is
strongly suspected of murdering a number of rich widows.
He seeks sanctuary with his brother and niece, also called
Charlie (Teresa Wright), in the small town of Santa Rosa.
Gradually Charlie develops her own suspicions of the uncle
she adores, and was named after. Charlie is also friendly with
a detective (Macdonald Carey) who also entertains a 'shadow
of a doubt' about the amiable Uncle Charlie. Gradually,
Uncle Charlie grows aware of his niece's suspicions and twice
tries to kill her, lest she reveals her suspicions and betrays
him. His last attempt fails, and he himself falls in front of an

oncoming train. The girl keeps the secret to herself as Santa Rosa turns out to pay tribute to the memory of good old Uncle Charlie!

The rich irony of the plot obviously appealed to Hitchcock, as did the idea of menace under the veneer of all that is good about small-town America. It was also an idea that Orson Welles developed in *The Stranger* (1946), where he played a Nazi war criminal sheltering in a similarly 'nice' town. The redoubtable American film critic James Agee was a long-time admirer of Hitchcock's work. Agee's film reviews in *Time* and *The Nation* were called by W H Auden 'the most remarkable regular event in American journalism today.' Agee wrote that *Shadow of a Doubt* was an 'interesting picture . . . with some real attention to what places and people really look like in Santa Rosa.'

Shadow of a Doubt was developed from a novel by Gordon McDonell. Hitchcock was pleased that the eminent American playwright and novelist Thornton Wilder collaborated on the screenplay alongside Alma; Wilder had established himself as the Poet Laureate of Americana with his 1938 play *Our Town*. Hitchcock confided to Truffaut that in his English days he was quite used to notable writers working on his films, but in America he felt that the more eminent the writer, the more they looked down their nose at him and his films. His joy was twofold; not only was he happy to secure Wilder, he also enjoyed working with him.

Hitchcock was also blessed with a particularly strong cast for *Shadow*. Teresa Wright had won an Oscar just the year before for her role in *Mrs Miniver* and was ideal for the role of a young niece devoted to her uncle but having terrible doubts about her misplaced devotion; this split in character and gradual disillusionment was sharply portrayed. Notable among the supporting cast were Henry Travers (as Charlie's father) and Hume Cronyn as his neighbor. They shared an unhealthy obsession with grisly murder mysteries, blithely unaware that one was taking place right beneath their noses.

The pivotal role of Uncle Charlie was ideally suited to Joseph Cotten. Cotten was 37 at the time and, directed by his long-time friend Orson Welles, had already appeared in two of the finest-ever American sound films, *Citizen Kane* and *The Magnificent Ambersons*. By the mid-1940s Cotten was in the front rank of American screen actors, and his onscreen amiability disguised a deeper, richer screen persona, which – as he had done with Cary Grant in *Suspicion* – Hitchcock tapped. Everyone loves Uncle Charlie, and Cotten fitted the role like a glove, a friendly word for everyone, nothing but praise for his sister's cooking, and a fund of anecdotes for the family. It is by small, obsessive details that Hitchcock allows Teresa Wright to spot her uncle's feet of clay, which ultimately leads to his death.

Below: *Young Charlie's doubts grow about her 'kindly uncle.'*

Above: *Teresa Wright and Macdonald Carey in a publicity shot from* Shadow of a Doubt.

Much of *Shadow of a Doubt* finds Hitchcock in the territory which director Frank Capra made his own – touching, affectionate portrayals of small-town America. Capra saw these backwaters as the backbone of the nation, personified by the indomitability and uncommon ordinariness of James Stewart. The film also allows Hitchcock to build further on elements which had asserted themselves in his earlier works – surely nothing terrible could happen in Santa Rosa, surely Uncle Charlie could not be a murderer? The whole film is a sleight of hand. Underneath the wholesomeness of the town lies a terrible doubt, emphasized by Cotten's entry into Santa Rosa: Hitchcock insisted that the train carrying the character should be seen belching black smoke in the sunshine, as if to imply that the train was carrying evil incarnate.

Hitchcock was allowed to use Cotten the villain as his central character (a device he was to use again in *Stage Fright* and *Psycho*) but only because no matter how strongly it is implied that he murdered these rich widows the audience never actually sees him murder them, as this would totally alienate the sympathy for Uncle Charlie which must be sustained right up to the film's conclusion.

Hitchcock was pleased to normalize his central character in *Shadow of a Doubt*, stating that the 'villains are not all black and heroes are not all white; there are greys everywhere.' Throughout his career Hitchcock was keen to undermine his audience's moral cognisance, forcing them to identify with the most unlikely people: Norman Bates in *Psycho*, Bob Rusk in *Frenzy* and Bruno Anthony in *Strangers on a Train*. Hitchcock always enjoyed taking his audience to the limit, but took a special delight in making them care enough to sympathize with such unsavory characters. It is his appreciation of these grey areas of morality which makes Hitchcock such a fascinating director.

Shadow of a Doubt presented such an affectionate and authentic picture of small-town America that it is hard to believe Hitchcock had been working in the country for a mere four years when it was made. But then Hitchcock always had the ability to make his own world wherever he worked. As Sheridan Morley wrote: 'The truth was that Hitchcock . . . like Chaplin, inhabited and photographed a world of his own, one which had no more to do with Hollywood than it had ever really had to do with London.' Hitchcock's world is clearly his own and peculiarly timeless; the England of *Rebecca* and *Suspicion* is untouched by war, the San Francisco of *Vertigo* is a city in aspic and the inhabitants of the London of *Frenzy* look as though they have never heard of The Beatles!

Taking to the limits his ability to manufacture a self-contained but convincing world, Hitchcock narrowed focus even more for his next film. *Saboteur* spanned the USA, *Shadow of a Doubt* zeroed in on a small American town and *Lifeboat* (1943) centered on just one set, the vessel of the title. *Lifeboat* confined itself to one of the smallest acting spaces of any film ever made. Hitchcock saw the potential as 'a challenge . . . a microcosm of war.' The war in question was not going well for the Allies, America was suffering terrible setbacks in the Pacific, and the war in the West was all but at a stalemate. True, the Russians had halted the German advance at the gates of Moscow and the Nazis had suffered a terrible defeat at Stalingrad, but the Second Front that Stalin demanded was still nowhere to be seen. Churchill was terrified of the overwhelming success of the U-Boat packs in the Atlantic – in March 1943 alone 477,000 tons of Allied shipping had been sunk with only 12 U-Boats destroyed. With Britain and America finally allies, a lifeline across the Atlantic was essential to keep supplies pouring into England, from where the Allied invasion of Europe had to be launched.

Hitchcock was attracted by a John Steinbeck short story about the survivors of a torpedoed merchant ship, and their struggle for survival on a lifeboat. Cinematically the film presented a challenge, as all the 'action' had to take place in the boat. It was a challenge to which Hitchcock enthusiastically responded (as he had done with the introduction of sound 14 years before and was to do with *Rope* and *Rear Window* years later when he tackled the idea of a full length feature film taking place on just one set, but allowing full rein to the cinematic possibilities rather than regressing to the proscenium stage).

Above: *Heather Angel and Hume Cronyn in a publicity shot for* Lifeboat *(1943).*
Below: *The cast prepare for a grisly operation on board.*

Top: *Another crisis on the lifeboat.*
Above: *William Bendix reading the paper carrying Hitchcock's cleverest cameo role.*

The survivors fill up the lifeboat – a few members of the crew, an army nurse, a fashion writer and a millionaire. They then pick up one of the crew of the U-Boat which torpedoed them. Gradually, thanks to superior seamanship, the Nazi assumes command of the boat and is secretly steering it toward a German supply ship. The wounded seaman discovers his plan and is killed by the Nazi. The remaining survivors guess that the crewman's death was not suicide and kill the Nazi before being rescued by an Allied vessel at the last minute.

The whole thing was remarkably unlike Hitchcock's other work. It was an opportunity to study various types of people under pressure, to examine the psychology of the individual and to debate the morality of war. Hardly the sort of fodder the world had come to expect from 'The Master of Suspense.' But the world was at war, and Hitchcock would have been ignoring his responsibilities as an artist if he did not comment on the global struggle. The film's message according to Hitchcock was 'a statement telling the democracies to put their differences aside temporarily and to gather their forces to concentrate on the common enemy, whose strength was precisely derived from a spirit of unity and determination.' Indeed, the film's most responsible character is the Nazi, played by Walter Slezak. He is callous, precise, determined and methodical – exactly the qualities which had enabled the armed forces of Hitler's Reich to overrun Europe. It was Slezak's portrayal and Hitchcock's depiction which saw the film run into criticism: the critics apparently felt that a nasty Nazi could not be a good sailor! It was precisely that sympathetic portrayal of a German which caused Michael Powell and Emeric Pressburger such problems with their epic film *The Life and Death of Colonel Blimp* (1943), which was effectively banned by Churchill.

Despite the excellent playing of Slezak as the Nazi and John Hodiak and William Bendix as the seamen, Hitchcock agrees that the film was 'dominated' by Tallulah Bankhead as the fashion writer. Tallulah was notorious as one of the acting world's greatest characters and whatever role she took she reduced it to a quivering jelly thanks to her larger-than-life persona. However her natural exuberance and *joie de vivre* were never fully captured on film, and *Lifeboat* remains arguably her finest film role. She had no high opinion of her own beauty however and once cracked: 'They used to photograph Shirley Temple through gauze. They should photograph me through linoleum!'

In order to emphasize the isolation of the lifeboat situation, Hitchcock never let his cameras leave their environment; nor did he have any music on the film's soundtrack to distract his audience. Such starkness, and the criticisms of the 'good Nazi,' did not help the film at the box office, but nevertheless Hitchcock felt that he had benefitted from the experience of working in such a deliberately claustrophobic set. He also hugely enjoyed his own cameo appearance: obviously a lifeboat with only nine survivors left little room for a passing appearance from the film's director. At one point Hitch toyed with the idea of floating past as a corpse, but the studio deemed this too macabre, and Hitchcock was also afraid he

Below: *The legendary Salvador Dali in front of his set design for* Spellbound *(1945).*

would drown. So he appeared as the 'Before and After' man in a slimming advertisement in a newspaper read by one of the crew, and consequently found himself inundated by zealous dieters desperate to obtain the fictional 'Reduco'!

Lifeboat is an incongruous Hitchcock film but, as with all his films, there are many elements to enjoy and admire. Obviously, the actors dominate this film (the Cattle for whom Hitchcock did in fact have a grudging respect). The tragedies and ironies of war are discussed and the social barriers break down (later also tackled in a much lighter vein in the 1957 *The Admirable Crichton*). However the characters were just not as sympathetic as Allied propagandists would have wished. Their calculated murder of the Nazi who had helped save their lives was balanced by Slezak's cold-blooded murder of the crewman who had unearthed his secret. As a 'microcosm of war' *Lifeboat* was effective, but hindsight reveals manifest flaws and it lacks the broad sweep of *Blimp* and, indeed, that film's durability and invention. Technically however *Lifeboat* stands up well and it is a testament to Hitchcock's fluency that he can make a single-set film grip the audience throughout. Perhaps it is not too fanciful to see in the gallery of types flung together in adversity the seeds for the disaster movie genre of the 1970s.

Talking of Alfred Hitchcock's American work, and *Lifeboat* in particular, James Agee commented: 'The handling of the cinematic problems is extremely astute, in spite of a smell of the studio about most of it . . . What disturbs me is the question of whether Hitchcock recognizes . . . he has at last become so engrossed in the solution of pure problems of technique that he has lost some of his sensitiveness toward the purely human aspects of what he is doing. . . . In his finest films he has always shown, always cinematically, qualities of judgment and perception which, to my mind, bring him abreast of all but the best writers of his time . . .'

The London to which Alfred Hitchcock returned in spring 1944 was a bruised and battered city after five long years of war. Hitchcock spent over six months in the capital working on several projects for the Ministry of Information and took the opportunity to renew some old acquaintances. One of the people Hitchcock was pleased to be working with again was Angus MacPhail, who many years before had told him about the MacGuffin. The two men had known each other since working together on *The Lodger* in 1926 and now, alongside their war work, took the opportunity to collaborate once again. The basic plot outline they worked on was to become Hitchcock's next feature film, *Spellbound* (1945).

On returning to America, Hitchcock worked with Ben Hecht on the final screenplay. Hecht, with Charles Mac-Arthur, had written *the* classic play on the ethics of journalism, *The Front Page*, and had helped shape Emily Brontë's *Wuthering Heights* for the screen in 1939 – without even bothering to read the novel! Hecht shared Hitchcock's growing interest in psychoanalysis and together they managed to turn Francis Beeding's novel *The House of Doctor Edwardes* into *Spellbound*. The novel literally features lunatics

Right: *Ben Hecht worked on the screenplay of* Spellbound *and* Notorious *(1946)*.
Below and opposite: *Dali's surreal set for* Spellbound, *in the planning stage and on film.*

taking over the asylum and from it Hitchcock and Hecht fashioned a psychological thriller. Ingrid Bergman plays Constance Peterson, a doctor at a mental home who falls in love with the institution's new head, John Ballantyne (Gregory Peck). Bergman eventually discovers that Peck is an amnesiac who has assumed the identity of the real doctor, whom he believes he has murdered. She is convinced that he is not a murderer and forces him to undergo psychoanalysis, which reveals that he has always felt responsible for the accidental death of his brother, and recently witnessed the death of Dr Edwardes, which left him feeling equally guilty. However Edwardes' death was not an accident, but cold-blooded murder, ironically committed by the long-standing head of the asylum Dr Murchison (Leo G Carroll) who was about to be replaced by Edwardes. The film ends happily with Bergman unmasking the real murderer and departing for a life of guilt-free bliss with the cured Peck.

There are many familiar echoes from earlier Hitchcock works: the threatened hero befriended and helped by the heroine, the innocent man on the run, the guilty man disguising his tracks and making the evidence point to the innocent, and the innocent man having to evade the police for long enough to discover the truth and clear his own name. What makes *Spellbound* so distinctive is Hitchcock's detailed build up of the characters, particularly Peck's. The film's most famous scene has Peck undergoing analysis, probing his subconscious and revealing his dreams and neuroses. Freud's pioneering work into the human subconscious was

Above: *Original publicity poster for* Spellbound.

still fresh in people's minds; his landmark work *Interpretation of Dreams* was published only in 1900, and psychiatry was a branch of medicine few yet took seriously or fully understood. It was thanks to Ben Hecht that such heady ideas were transformed into an intelligible, fluent screenplay, but it was Hitchcock's visual genius which made those dreams take form on the cinema screen. These days with surreal pop videos on television every few minutes it is hard to appreciate the impact which the dream sequence in *Spellbound* had on cinema audiences in 1945.

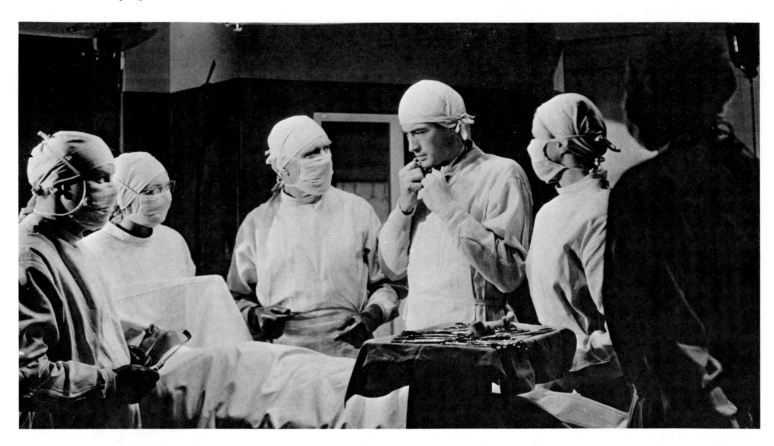

Top: *Gregory Peck is unmasked in* Spellbound, *and* (above) *with the concerned and loving psychiatrist, Ingrid Bergman.*

To fully visualize Peck's tormented dreams Hitchcock asked Salvador Dali to collaborate on the sequence. Dali was by then one of the world's most famous artists, and no stranger to the cinema. His collaborations with Luis Buñuel on *Un Chien Andalou* (1928) and *L'Age D'or* (1930) were legendary and while some, George Orwell among them, decried Dali's grotesque imagination, few would deny his craftsmanship or wealth of visual ideas. Indeed Dali seemed an ideal choice for the film as he had always maintained that his work could only be appreciated by the unconscious, which fitted in with Hitchcock's aim for the dream sequence. Hitchcock wanted clarity and visual sharpness in *Spellbound*, a complete break with the Hollywood tradition of handling cinematic dreams by shooting them opaquely, blurred and out of focus. Hitchcock was keen to shoot the Dali scenes out of doors using natural light to aid the clarity, but the studios balked, and they were eventually shot on massive indoor stages. Dali scholars recognized the artist's symbols – the knife waved before the eye, the crooked wheels, faceless men, distorted perspectives, interminable vistas populated by incongruous objects. To this day those sequences retain their power to disturb and unsettle – exactly the effect Hitchcock was looking for.

Hitchcock, perhaps embarrassed by his own interest in such things, dismisses *Spellbound* rather lightly as 'Just another manhunt story wrapped up in pseudo-psychoanalysis.' Similarly Orson Welles had felt that the superficial psychological aspect of *Citizen Kane* was nothing more than 'dime store Freud.' An early title in the film states that the point of psychoanalysis is to 'open the locked doors of the mind.' *Spellbound* attempts this but gets bogged down by too much psychoanalytic gobbledegook, with the principal actors forced to utter such lines as 'That's a delusion you have, acquired out of illness . . .' and 'You taught me what Freud said . . .' James Agee too found it flawed, calling it, 'Hitchcock's surprisingly disturbing thriller about psychoanalysis' and criticized the 'none too interesting murder mystery which merely cheapened and got in the way of any possible psychological interest.' Some may say that for Alfred Hitchcock it was the psychological interest which got in the way of a rather unusual murder mystery!

Leo G Carroll, a great favorite of the director's, was here in a rare villainous role as Dr Murchison; altogether he appeared in six Hitchcock films, more than any other actor, although he is still probably best remembered today as Mr Waverley in the 1960s TV serial *The Man from UNCLE*. Carroll's regular appearances in Hitchcock's American films were symptomatic of the director's constant use of British actors in predominantly American settings. It may seem incongruous that such recognizably English actors appear for no apparent reason in roles which should have gone to their US counterparts – think of Sir Cedric Hardwicke in *Rope*, Anthony Quayle in *The Wrong Man*, and most unusually Carroll as a US senator in *Strangers on a Train*.

Ingrid Bergman as Dr Peterson was at the peak of her career, she had won the Oscar for her performance in *Gaslight* (1944), and was to be forever remembered as Ilse in Michael Curtiz' all-time great *Casablanca*. Working for the first time with Hitchcock, Bergman recalled a telling example of the director's attitude to his cast. She felt that in one scene she could not play it 'naturally' and went on to detail to Hitchcock her reservations about the psychological imbalance which she felt made her character's actions incongruous. He listened in silence and then responded, 'All right Ingrid, if you can't do it naturally, then *fake* it.' Despite such differences of opinion, Bergman is perfect as Dr Peterson, showing beautifully the split between her professional face as a 'human glacier' and the passionate woman in love with Gregory Peck.

Still a newcomer at the time of *Spellbound*, for which he received good notices, Peck's real success was still to come. Hitchcock was never enamored of Peck but although he is saddled with the role of an amnesiac schizophrenic with a guilt complex who also has to carry the main love interest Peck delivers an intense performance.

Spellbound restored Hitchcock's name at the box office, making a satisfactory $7 million for the studio. Allowed a free rein with Dali, it was also a largely pleasurable experience for Hitchcock. He enjoyed working with Ingrid Bergman (whose box-office appeal could not be denied) and was only too delighted to work with her again on his next proper film *Notorious* (1946).

By 1945 the war in Europe was coming to a close. Mention should be made of Hitchcock's largely unrecognized work on a series of propaganda films which he made specifically to help the war effort. Hitchcock had made the perilous wartime Transatlantic flight crammed into the belly of a bomber, and on arrival in London contacted Sidney Bernstein, his old friend from the 1920s. Bernstein later went on to found Britain's Granada TV, as well as producing two of Hitchcock's postwar films – the classic *Rope* (1948) and *Under Capricorn* (1949) – but at that time was working on the Psychological Warfare Division of the Supreme Headquarters Allied Expeditionary Forces (SHAEF). At Bernstein's request, Hitchcock undertook two short films for the Ministry of Information (MOI) in 1944. *Bon Voyage* told of the work of the French Resistance and how they abetted the escape of a shot-down RAF pilot, while *Aventure Malgaché* concentrated on the divisions within the Free French forces

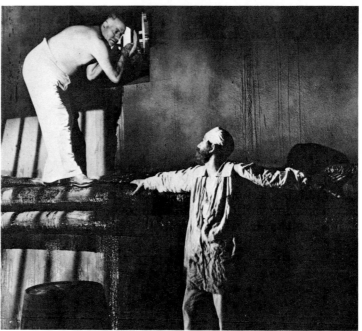

Top: *Bergman begins unravelling her lover's psyche.*
Above: *Scene from Hitchcock's 1944 propaganda short* Aventure Malgaché.

during the time leading up to Liberation. Both films featured the Molière Players, then working with the Free French in exile in London.

Hitchcock's most potentially significant propaganda effort lay unseen in the vaults of the Imperial War Museum in London for 40 years: five reels of film which showed the horrifying truth about the Nazi death camps. Bernstein ordered a Ministry of Information film crew into Belsen three days after Liberation to film the monstrous aftermath of the Holocaust. When the full horror of this one camp was revealed, Bernstein accumulated hundreds of thousands of feet of film from the 5000 other camps. Bernstein's idea was that the film be 'an objective report, which would demonstrate the terror methods used by the Germans . . . in the form of a prosecuting counsel setting his case.' But on seeing the footage MOI were concerned that it might have a

Opposite: *A member of the Molière Players in Ministry of Information short* Bon Voyage *(1944), which Hitchcock filmed on a wartime visit to London.*
Above: *Survivors of the Nazi holocaust. Hitchcock edited footage of the holocaust; it was so horrific that it remained unshown for 40 years.*

'boomerang effect, since the public might query its authenticity.' Bernstein therefore engaged Colin Wills of the *News Chronicle* and Richard Crossman to work on a script, and Solly Zuckerman was called in as Scientific and Medical Advisor. Bernstein recalled: 'When the first film started coming in, I realized it needed some completely objective editing. So I called in Hitchcock.' Hitchcock was installed in his suite at Claridge's and he began watching the footage: 'Hitchcock sent out some instructions to the cameramen; for example, ensuring authenticity, that the cameramen take long tracking shots so they could not be interfered with. He saw all the film as it came in, but didn't like looking at it.'

It was no surprise that Hitchcock, the screen's most effectively chilling director, could hardly bear to watch the footage as it flooded in. This was more horrifying than any fiction culled from a writer's mind. Corpses were flung like pathetic rag dolls into mass graves, the faces of the corpses are reminiscent of the Hell painted by Bosch, but far, far worse. These were pitiful corpses of real people who had been living ordinary lives before Hitler's pestilent regime infected Europe. Postwar apologists for the Nazi regime claim the Holocaust never happened – this film is the awful proof that it did happen and must never be forgotten or allowed to happen again. Hitchcock's methods of verifying the authenticity of

the film included the use of panning and tracking shots, depicting the mounds of bodies, with no cuts to prove that there had been no technical trickery, and that these awful images were undeniably *real*. He cut from the mounds of unidentifiable bodies to the easily recognizable corpulent figures of local dignitaries and burgomasters in order to emphasize the idea of collective guilt. To try and show the scale of the atrocities Hitchcock used shots showing the piles of the victims' pitiful possessions – mountains of glasses, false teeth, toys and handbags. Finally, Hitchcock insisted that there be shots of the residential areas surrounding the death camps, to show the normality of the countryside, highlighting the iniquity of the murder factories and their proximity to ordinary people who may have wished to deny their existence.

Hitchcock, Bernstein and a team of editors had spent five harrowing months working on the most awful footage imaginable to produce just under an hour of film. The result was deemed too terrifying to be screened. The idea had been to show it to citizens in Germany to prove how foul the Nazi regime had been and to remind Allied audiences just what they had spent six long years fighting against. But such was the harrowing impact of the assembled footage that it was shelved and not screened until it was shown on British television in 1985 under the title *A Painful Reminder*. On this occasion the original commentary script was recorded for the first time and Bernstein's memories of the film were interspersed with the footage. Without doubt it is the most terrifying and powerful film Hitchcock's name was ever attached to; the names of Auschwitz, Belsen, Buchenwald, Dachau form an awful litany which condemns the Nazi regime for all eternity. Hitchcock remained deeply upset about the footage and never spoke openly about it.

Ingrid Bergman, revealed as a spy in Notorious *(1946), realizes her coffee has been drugged.*

PERFECTING THE ART

'For more than a year, Hitchcock had wanted to make a film about a man in love with a girl who, in the course of her official duties, had to go to bed with another man and eventually marry him,' wrote Cary Grant's biographer Geoffrey Wansell. With subsequent detours, that idea became *Notorious* (1946), one of Hitchcock's most stylish thrillers.

The film gave Hitchcock the opportunity to work again with Cary Grant and Ingrid Bergman, whom he admired for her ability to seem sexually attractive and distant at the same time. Producer Selznick was on hand again and predictably claimed the lion's share of inspiration: '*Notorious* was entirely my conception,' he announced in one of his innumerable memos, 'I did the script with Hitchcock and Ben Hecht, and prepared it for Ingrid Bergman and Cary Grant ... Increasingly, I learned to have great respect for Hitchcock. Thus, while I was working very closely with him on preparation, and while he left the editing to me, I left him entirely alone on the set.' This was a welcome change from the atmosphere while filming *Rebecca*, and indicative of the trust both men felt for each other, and for no one else. *Notorious* also marked the beginning of a fruitful collaboration with Edith Head, the legendary costume designer, who by the end of her career had acquired an astonishing eight Oscars. She worked on a total of 11 Hitchcock films over 30 years and had a high regard for his appreciation of color, which she said was as important 'as any painter's.'

Left: *Ingrid Bergman joins fellow spy Cary Grant for a tense drink in* Notorious *(1946), one of Hitchcock's most stylish thrillers.*
Below: *Bergman and Grant flying down to Rio.*

A London National Film Theatre program note called *Notorious* 'one of the most moving and disturbing accounts of the vicissitudes of heterosexual love that the cinema has produced.' In the film Bergman plays the daughter of an American Nazi sympathizer in postwar Brazil, where she has been dispatched by an FBI agent (Cary Grant) to spy on a gang of neo-Nazis. The Nazis are led by Alexander Sebastian (Claude Rains), who at Grant's insistence she eventually marries. Bergman discovers that the Nazis are plotting to build an atom bomb and is slowly poisoned by her husband, only to be rescued by Cary Grant at the very end, leaving Claude Rains to face death at the hands of his Nazi cohorts.

The passion in the love scenes between Grant and Bergman in their first film together is remarkable, as is Claude Rains' chilling portrayal of the villainous but strangely sympathetic Alex. The ruthlessness of Grant's Svengali to Bergman's Trilby is deftly handled in Ben Hecht's literate script, but before his manipulation comes to the fore, there is a marvelously charged love scene between the two. At the time the moral arbiters of Hollywood insisted that no screen kiss should last longer than three seconds. Bergman recalled the scene which became notorious itself, for having Hollywood's longest screen kiss: 'We just kissed each other and talked, leaned away and kissed each other again. Then the telephone came between us, and then we moved to the other side of the telephone. So it was a kiss which opened and closed: but the censors didn't cut the scene because we never at any point kissed for more than three seconds. We did other things, we nibbled each other's ears and kissed a cheek so that it looked endless and became sensational in Hollywood.' The love story between Grant and Bergman is sensitively handled,

Above: *The drugged coffee takes effect in* Notorious.

with Bergman as the idealistic young girl 'a nice unspoilt child whose heart is full of daisies and buttercups' as she cloyingly describes herself to the distant Grant.

It is, ironically, the villainous Claude Rains who comes across as a far nicer and more loving character than Grant's Devlin. Hitchcock's original choice for the role of Alex was the urbane Clifton Webb but in the event Claude Rains was ideal casting, sadly only making this one film with Hitchcock. Prior to *Notorious* he had secured a reputation as one of Hollywood's most durable and compelling character actors, with memorably villainous performances in *The Adventures of Robin Hood* and *Casablanca*. Along with Ben Hecht, Rains received an Academy Award nomination for his work on *Notorious*.

The film recalls *Rebecca* in more ways than one. Hitchcock assuredly details a love story, again with genuine characters filling the central roles, but this is an even darker romance than that which haunted Manderley. Hitchcock again brings out the darker side of Grant, who for the bulk of the film is seen to be simply using Bergman. Grant is portrayed as a callous, conniving, unsympathetic character and only in his final rescue of Bergman is he redeemed. The final third of the film has Bergman held captive in her husband's house, a lavish mansion in Rio, populated by an unwholesome collection of villains, including Ivan Triesault as the Nazi hitman and Leopoldine Konstantin – in her only American film role – as Alex's stern mother.

The film opens with a party. Bergman's father has been sentenced to 20 years' imprisonment and she is clearly drunk. Her first line to Cary Grant says it all, 'How about you handsome?' Unnervingly, the scene turns up again nearly 40 years later in Carl Reiner's elegant pastiche of private-eye movies *Dead Men Don't Wear Plaid* (1982) with Bergman's line cleverly addressed to Steve Martin.

The most exciting scene in the film is another party. Grant, desperate to learn what Rains is keeping so jealously guarded in his wine cellar, orders Bergman to obtain the key for him. As the party begins, Bergman is seen greeting guests in the lobby and in an astounding piece of technical virtuosity, recalling the similarly audacious shot in *Young and Innocent* 10 years before, Hitchcock's camera slowly swoops down from the ceiling, taking in the full panoply of the party, finally focussing on Bergman's hand nervously clutching the key. It is an assured, bravura piece of cinema, with Hitchcock ensuring that the audience's attention remains glued to the key to the plot. Later in the party, when Bergman and Grant have crept away to the mysterious wine cellar, all the suspense hinges on whether the champagne will run out, thereby causing Rains to descend and discover them unearthing his secret. So the suspense of the scene hinges on how many bottles of champagne the guests will consume.

The MacGuffin for *Notorious* was one that caused Hitchcock considerable problems at the time, but which in hindsight puts the film way ahead of its time. Originally Hecht and Hitchcock thought the MacGuffin at the film's center might concern the theft of diamonds, or the training of secret Nazi armies in the jungles of Brazil. But one was too mundane, and the other too costly, so they came up with the idea of uranium being stored in the wine bottles in Rains' cellar. At this time the truth about atomic warfare was largely unknown. Hitchcock had learned of the work being carried out under the strictest secrecy at Los Alamos, New Mexico, where scientists were beavering away to 'perfect' the atom bomb. Hitchcock and Hecht visited the California Institute of Technology and talked over the actual size and constituents of an atom bomb with scientists, but were only fobbed off with vagueness. Hitchcock always felt that the MacGuffin was simply the *flavor* of the plot, and never allowed mere details to intrude, so he pursued his vague idea that uranium had something to do with the manufacture of atom bombs and the finished film has Cary Grant finding some sand in a wine bottle. He takes it away for examination and later reveals to Bergman that it is uranium and asks her to find out where the Nazis are mining it. At no point is the bomb mentioned but Hitchcock's inquiries were sufficient to have him trailed for three months by the FBI following his visit to the Institute.

Notorious was a great critical and commercial success. In its review *Theater Arts* magazine said: 'With a highly polished script by Ben Hecht, and with Ingrid Bergman and Cary Grant to bring glamor and sultry vitality to the leads, Mr Hitchcock has fashioned a film in the supercharged American idiom of the sort that made *Casablanca* popular.' With such eulogies, Alfred Hitchcock had emphatically made his mark as a Hollywood director. *Variety* confirmed this: 'The production and directorial skill of Alfred Hitchcock combine with a suspenseful story and excellent performances to make *Notorious* forceful entertainment . . . The terrific suspense maintained to the very last is also an important asset.' Made for just under $2 million, the film took over $9 million within a year of its release.

Hitchcock had been a 'stranger in a strange land' for six years, and with the release of *Notorious*, his ninth film of that period, his assimilation was complete. The wartime trips to Britain had been depressing experiences; whole chunks of his boyhood city lay in ruins. The shots of the Old Bailey court-house in *The Paradine Case* (1947), for example, look like a giant wedding cake with a slice missing. There was a grim determination in the indomitable 'Blitz spirit' of Londoners but after the paradise of California, with no blackout or rationing, London seemed a dark and depressing place. Coupled with his grisly work on the concentration camp footage, Hitchcock was only too glad to return to California, although he retained for the rest of his life an affection for England and London in particular.

During his English period Hitchcock had a fondness for real location work (exemplified by *Blackmail* and *The 39 Steps*) and often used foreign scouting trips as impromptu family holidays. Later, however, he came to rely increasingly on studios to create his own worlds. He told Truffaut in 1972, when asked the difference between UK and US studios: 'When I enter the studios – be it in Hollywood or in London – and the heavy doors close behind me, there is no difference. A coal mine is always a coal mine!' It was within the confines of that 'coal mine' that Hitchcock created his own worlds. As John Russell Taylor wrote: 'Hitch's landscape always has been a landscape of fantasy. All that counts is the intensity and conviction of the fantasy.'

Above: *Bergman's duped husband Alexander (Claude Rains) and his mother (Leopoldine Konstantin) plan their next move.*
Below left: *Cary Grant finally rescues his love, leaving Claude Rains to his fate.*

It is fascinating to read George Orwell's essay *Decline of the English Murder*, which was published in 1946 – the same year that *Notorious* was released. It brilliantly evokes the very English world which Hitchcock was so adept at creating in his films. Orwell's essay blissfully conjures up a contented middle-class household between the wars. After a traditional Sunday lunch, the husband settles down in front of the fire with a pot of tea and a bulging pipe, to read a juicy murder story in the *News of the World*. Orwell defines the 'great period in murder' as being between 1850 and 1925, with sex and money as the prime motives: 'With all this in mind, we can construct what would be, from the *News of the World* reader's point of view, the "perfect murder". The murderer should be a little man of the professional class – a dentist or solicitor say – living an immensely respectable life somewhere in the suburbs, and preferably in a semi-detached house, which will allow the neighbours to hear suspicious sounds through the wall. He should either be Chairman of the local Conservative Party branch, or a leading Nonconformist and strong Temperance advocate. He should go astray through cherishing a guilty passion for his secretary or the wife of a rival professional man, and should only bring himself to the point of murder after long and terrible wrestles with his conscience. Having decided on murder, he should plan it all with the utmost cunning, and only slip up over some tiny unforeseen detail. The means chosen, of course, should be poison. In the last analysis he should commit murder because this seems to him less disgraceful, and less damaging to his career, than being detected in adultery. With this kind of background, a crime can have dramatic and even tragic qualities which make it memorable and excite pity for both victim and murderer!' This pity for the murderer as well as for the victim finds resonance in Hitchcock's best work, functioning in that gray moral halflight of which he was always so fond.

Above: *Hitchcock's cameo alongside Gregory Peck in* The Paradine Case *(1947).*

Hitchcock chose to return to his native England for the setting of his next film, *The Paradine Case* (1947), but he preferred to re-create it from memory, remaining in America and shooting it largely in the studio. This was to be his last film for Selznick after a fruitful seven-year contract. The film was based on a novel by Robert Hichens and the screenplay was by Selznick and Alma. Selznick had in fact originally purchased the property in 1933 as a vehicle for Greta Garbo, considering her ideal for the mysterious Mrs Paradine, and had intended to put John Barrymore, Lionel Barrymore and Diana Wynyard in the roles later taken by Gregory Peck, Charles Laughton and Ann Todd. He noted in 1946 that 'unfortunately, Miss Garbo has always had an aversion to the story, and even today won't play it.' It was a role ideally suited to the enigmatic Garbo; as Charles Coburn remarks of Mrs Paradine in the film, 'You'll find her a strange woman with an almost mystic calm.'

The story concerns Mrs Paradine (Alida Valli) who is standing trial for the murder of her blind husband. She denies it, but during her trial, it emerges that she has been having an affair with her husband's valet (Louis Jourdan). Mrs Paradine's defense counsel Anthony Keane (Gregory Peck) meanwhile has fallen in love with her. His wife Gay (Ann Todd) is lusted after by the trial judge Horfield (Charles Laughton), who is contemptuous of her husband's performance in court. Trying to save his client's life, Peck manages to break down Louis Jourdan in the dock, causing his subsequent suicide. When she learns of her lover's death, Valli, broken hearted and with nothing left to live for, confesses in the dock that she did murder her husband and implies that Peck is in love with her. Peck quickly leaves the court in shame under Laughton's caustic eye, but the film ends with the knowledge that his long-suffering wife will stand by him.

What initially appealed to Hitchcock about the project was 'to take a person like Mrs Paradine, to put her in the hands of the police, to have her submit to all their formalities, and to say to her maid as she was leaving her home between the two Inspectors "I don't think I shall be back for dinner"!' The idea of a beautiful, upper-class woman's decline into degradation sustained Hitchcock's interest, although the central idea of Hichens' novel was, by 1947, terribly outdated, with Todd forced to utter such lines as 'Nice people don't go around murdering other nice people!'

Given its essentially static look the budget of $4 million was lavish. It is courtroom hokum, in truth far better handled by Billy Wilder in his *Witness For The Prosecution* (1957), in which Laughton virtually repeats his role and Marlene Dietrich is the alluring witness. But Hitchcock struggled gamely with *The Paradine Case*, even though he had severe doubts about Peck's suitability for the role of Keane. He would have preferred either Laurence Olivier or Ronald Colman for the role, and also felt that Louis Jourdan was far too smooth and urbane for the role of the groom/valet; his ideal casting for the role would, he enthusiastically told Truffaut, have been Robert Newton 'with horny hands, like the Devil!' Hitchcock was also unhappy about Valli as Mrs Paradine; *The Paradine*

Right: *Gregory Peck meets the mysterious Mrs Paradine (Alida Valli) for the first time.*
Below: *The uncomfortable dinner party with host Charles Laughton not in sight.*

Case was her first English language film, and her great triumph lay two years in the future with *The Third Man*. *The Paradine Case* marked the US debut of Todd, who had shot to fame as the distraught concert pianist playing alongside James Mason in *The Seventh Veil* (1945).

Another bonus for Hitchcock while making the film was the opportunity to work with Charles Laughton again, with Ethel Barrymore, the doyenne of the withering dynasty, as his

wife. Hitchcock once admitted ruefully, 'You can't direct a Laughton picture. The best you can hope for is to referee!' Laughton's performance as Judge Horfield was one of his few memorable acting roles since he had arrived in Hollywood with a bang. In the preceding decade he had been outstanding as Quasimodo in *The Hunchback of Notre Dame*, but in the ensuing years had squandered his talent in a number of B-movies. As Horfield he managed to humanize the monster and turned in a cameo of lethal spite and some poignancy. He coolly remarks at one stage, 'I do not like to be interrupted in the middle of an insult.' His treatment of his long-suffering wife in the film is despicable, as when he reminisces over dinner about an incident at Deauville: 'I managed to persuade Lady Millicent to go swimming at 70. I watched her frolicking in the surf and had sad thoughts about the impermanence of beauty.' When she pathetically wonders if Horfield can exercise mercy in his judgment, Laughton snaps, 'The Paradine woman will be hanged after three clear Sundays.' Laughton and Barrymore effortlessly stole the acting honors from the principals and remain one of the delights of *The Paradine Case*.

Despite Hitchcock's doubts, Selznick considered Gregory Peck to be 'the only star of importance in the film,' and, to his credit, Peck delivers an authoritative performance, particularly in the cross-examination scene where he breaks down Louis Jourdan's alibi, toying with him like a mongoose eyeing a snake.

Above: *Gregory Peck and long-suffering wife, played by Ann Todd.*
Below: *Peck cross-examines Louis Jourdan (right) in a courtroom scene from* The Paradine Case.

Opposite: *Lobby display for Hitchcock's masterpiece* Rope *(1948).*

From the desultory courtroom complexities of *The Paradine Case*, Hitchcock effortlessly moved on to make a masterpiece. *Rope* (1948) is exceptional for a number of reasons. It was Hitchcock's first film in color; it was the first film he had both produced and directed; and it was all to be shot in long 10-minute takes, a total break from filmmaking techniques of the time. Hitchcock had experimented with longer than average takes in *The Paradine Case*, but Selznick, feeling they were protracted and slowed down the action, broke down the scenes with close ups. *Rope* was also the start of a fruitful relationship with James Stewart, who went on to appear in three more Hitchcock films. *Rope* was budgeted at only $1½ million, most of which went on the technical side, with James Stewart's salary accounting for $300,000.

The film was based on a play by Patrick Hamilton, whose other filmed works were *Gaslight* (successfully filmed twice) and the atmospherically Gothic *Hangover Square*. Actor Hume Cronyn (who had made his screen debut in *Shadow of a Doubt* [1943]) helped Hitchcock with the adaptation, and additional dialogue was provided by the playwright Arthur Laurents, who went on to write *West Side Story* and *The Way We Were*. The story concerns two young bachelors (the chilling John Dall and weak Farley Granger) who strangle a friend for kicks, stuffing his body into a chest in their apartment, where later the same night they hold a dinner party, literally over his dead body! Among the guests are the dead boy's parents and the murderers' old college professor Rupert Cadell (James Stewart). Stewart's suspicions are aroused by the two men's guilty reactions, and he eventually discovers the body and turns the murderers over to the police.

While today *Rope* is fondly remembered for its technical achievements, the subtlety of the writing and performances is often overlooked. Stewart was already established as a major Hollywood star, with memorable performances in *The Philadelphia Story* (1940) and *It's a Wonderful Life* (1946) to his credit, but he had been away at war for three years and *Rope* helped re-establish his reputation as one of cinema's most versatile actors. Stewart's performance in *Rope* is a distinctive addition to his screen repertoire – as Cadell, he is world-weary and cynical, his onscreen amiability is replaced by a more mature and pensive character. Like Mrs Danvers in *Rebecca*, he suddenly materializes in the apartment, dispensing wit and wisdom until he realizes that his philosophies have been taken and grotesquely distorted by his two former students. Stewart's final scene as he discovers the body and realizes the two murderers took their inspiration from him is chilling in its intensity. His whole world crumbles and he is suddenly made ashamed of his every concept and idea, and rails at the boys, 'By what right do you *dare* to say there's a superior law?'

It is around these Nietzschean concepts that the film revolves. The elegantly sinister Dall literally sits at Stewart's feet, lapping up his theoretical nonsense about justifiable murder, and distorts it to his own criminal ends. The relationship between the two murderers is clearly homosexual, and Granger has the hapless, feminine role, panicking and flustered, while Dall (a recognized stage actor who sadly made few film appearances) is the calm, logical 'husband.' It is Dall who peppers his conversation with constant references to 'superior' and 'inferior' types and elevates murder into an

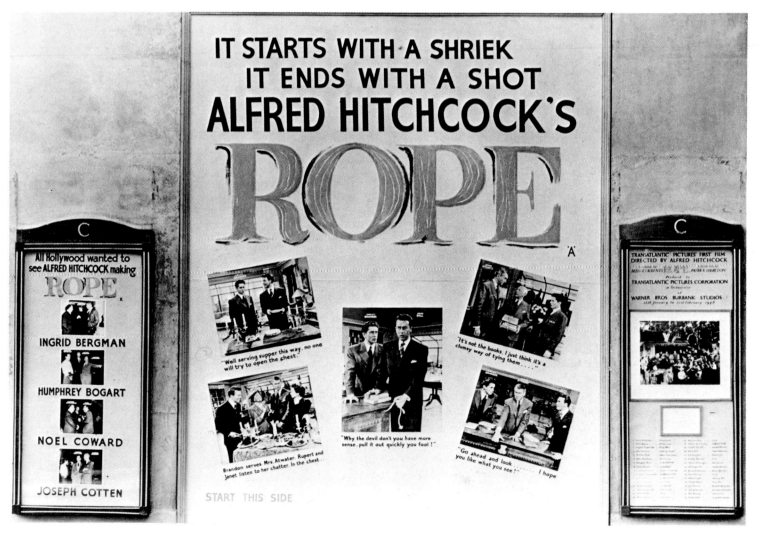

Above: *A macabre cocktail party at the beginning of* Rope.

art form: 'Moral concepts of right and wrong, of good and evil, don't hold for the intellectually superior.' He is contemptuous of weakness, admiring only strength and determination, and claims to recognize the inferiority of the many, and the superiority of the few: who by his warped standards should be able to dispose of their inferiors at their whim. Although this is the warped philosophy on which Hitler built his Third Reich, Dall has nothing but contempt for Nazis either, because of their stupidity. Dall is one of Hitchcock's genuinely repugnant villains, all the more so because of his onscreen grace and charm, which mask his contemptible views with an elegant and intellectual sheen. From early on you can sense his delight at having murdered, the almost sexual thrill of having killed, while wisecracking to the quivering Granger, 'Of course, he was a Harvard undergraduate, so it could be considered justifiable homicide!'

As the guests arrive, the script turns into a black comedy. The corpse lies still warm in a chest only a few feet away, while such lines as 'Oh you'll be the death of me . . .,' 'I hope you'll knock 'em dead' and 'Killing two birds with one stone . . .' take on a macabre significance, like the leitmotiv of 'knife' that Hitchcock built on in *Blackmail*.

Hamilton's play was rooted in the real-life Leopold and Loeb murder case of the 1920s, when two men killed an acquaintance for kicks, which was later filmed as *Compulsion* (1959). It is the killers' suavity and composure, their bravado, which is their undoing. Again, Hitchcock derives great suspense from the most unlikely source, as he did with the champagne consumption in *Notorious*. In *Rope* a tense scene revolves around the harmless figure of the housekeeper Mrs Wilson, busily clearing the top of the chest of crockery. She walks to and fro (seeming to take forever) between the chest and the kitchen, finally removing the cloth and about to lift the lid in order to fill the chest with books. All the while, an innocuous conversation goes on about the whereabouts of the victim, and the weather, but the audience is wholly mesmerized by the figure of the housekeeper, pottering on with her household chores.

Rope is successful on two levels. Intellectually it serves as an argument against the odium of Fascist theories, with a deftly

literate script milking the black humor of the situation at every occasion. Cedric Hardwicke's portrayal of the victim's father is especially touching, as we know that his only son is lying a few feet away, killed by his two callous contemporaries. There is a nice tongue-in-cheek sequence between Hardwicke's sister and the dead boy's girlfriend about film stars, 'The man I have a passion for is James Mason . . .,' 'So passionately sinister . . .,' then the conversation turns to the advantages of Errol Flynn over Cary Grant and the beauty of Ingrid Bergman! The second level where the film succeeds is purely technical. Hitchcock uses eight 10-minute takes to tell the story in an entirely cinematic but innovative method, with the action of the plot confined to the apartment and the actual length of the film. With hindsight Hitchcock admits that he was 'quite nonsensical' to tackle the film in that way, but in fact *Rope* stands up remarkably well nearly 40 years later.

The techniques employed in *Rope* are not only technically interesting, but also add a fluency and unencumbered style to what could otherwise have been a trite melodrama. The long shots take the audience in their care. *Rope* is a supreme achievement, with the only cuts (necessary to enable a magazine change) taking place when the camera fills the screen with a character's back or the chest. Now cross-cutting and fast editing seem to be a standard ploy in films of the thriller genre, the director believing that the quicker the cutting, the faster the action and the more the suspense builds up. Hitchcock demonstrated quite the opposite, most notably with the scene of Mrs Wilson and her lengthy trips to the kitchen, which takes the audience to the brink. Like Hitchcock, how-

Below: *Farley Granger (left) and John Dall concealing the body of their victim in a chest, from which dinner is later served.*

Above: *As night falls James Stewart discovers the murderers' 'perfect' crime.*

ever, Stewart had his doubts about the techniques employed: 'It wasn't altogether a success. The audiences wanted to be just audiences. They didn't really want to become the eyes of a mobile camera!'

The logistics of shooting *Rope* were awesome. Hitchcock undertook 10 days of intensive rehearsal with the cast and crew and the whole set had to be slotted together like some enormous doll's house, with movable walls and furniture to allow the camera freedom of movement. The lighting also posed a serious problem, as a realistic transition from early evening to dusk had to be achieved. The cast of course had to be word perfect, the camera had to flow smoothly. Filming the first scene, everything went perfectly for eight minutes, until at the very end as Dall and Granger stalked to the chest, a lighting cameraman was clearly visible standing by the window. It was, of course, traumatic; any number of things are liable to go wrong on a film set at the best of times, but in this case any minor flaw from a member of the cast or crew rendered an entire long sequence unusable. This put extra pressure on everyone concerned, for although the actors were well versed in stage techniques the immense technical apparatus multiplied the likelihood of mistakes.

Hitchcock had allowed himself to be confined to one set in *Lifeboat* five years before, but *Rope* was even more demanding. Four separate camera operators were credited and the entire film was shot in a remarkable 18 days, six of which were retakes because the lighting effects had turned out to be

unrealistic. The norm at that time was to see black-and-white rushes even for color films but luckily Hitchcock insisted on seeing his rushes in color, thus spotting the gaudy sky, which looked totally artificial early on. It is difficult to convey just how complex an undertaking *Rope* was; the very placing of characters needed a stage director's approach, while marshalling all the vast technical apparatus of film, would have tested the patience of a field marshal. In a normal film even a scene as simple as an exchange of dialogue between two characters has an establishing shot, detailing who the characters are, what they are wearing, what the location is. Then the camera cuts, usually, between the two characters as they speak, so that the average dialogue scene in a film would have more cuts than the whole of *Rope*. Most films are shot in sections lasting from two seconds to a matter of minutes, not necessarily chronologically, then edited together to produce the finished film. *Rope*, however, was shot as it was seen on screen.

At the time the film did seem too tricksy for the public and was not a great success commercially, although Hitchcock, as producer for the first time, was more than satisfied. It was only on its rerelease over 30 years later that the manifest strengths of the film revealed themselves, which make it ironically one of Hitchcock's most durable films.

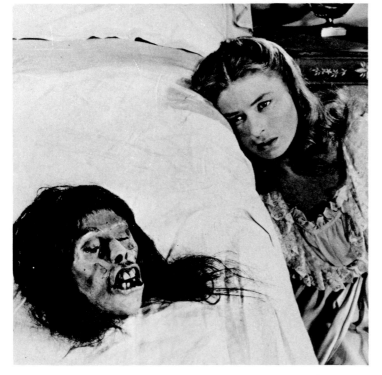

Above: *Ménage à trois in* Under Capricorn *(1949), (l to r) Margaret Leighton, Joseph Cotten and Ingrid Bergman.*
Left: *Bergman driven to the brink of insanity by strange bedfellow.*

Enjoying his independence, Hitchcock went straight on to make *Under Capricorn* (1949), which proved to be his final costume drama and received some of the worst notices of his career. Hitchcock made the mistake of believing that by landing Ingrid Bergman – at that time one of the top stars at the box office – he had ensured that at least all her fans would come flocking. But for *Under Capricorn* they stayed away in droves! Quite what attracted Hitchcock to Helen Simpson's novel about the strange goings-on in the Australia of the 1830s is hard to imagine. *Under Capricorn* is a rehash of the themes of *Rebecca*, with Bergman in the Joan Fontaine role as the young innocent trapped in a large, sinister house with a distant husband, and Margaret Leighton as a near-relative of Mrs Danvers. At best *Under Capricorn* is an unholy cross between *Rebecca* and *Jane Eyre*, with the three witches from *Macbeth* thrown into the kitchen for good measure. At its worst, it is a turgid historical potboiler. Only the critics of *Cahiers du Cinéma*, who revered Hitchcock during the 1950s, had a good word to say about the film. In *The Warner Brothers Story*, the authors bluntly call *Under Capricorn* 'a catastrophe at the box office . . . it was misconceived from the outset, and suffered from a talkative, badly resolved screenplay, as well as the miscasting of both Bergman and Cotten.' (Joseph Cotten witheringly referred to the film as 'Under Crapricorn.') Hitchcock was still preoccupied with the 10-minute takes he had pioneered in *Rope*, but in the context of *Under Capricorn* the long takes are clumsy and intrusive. Hitchcock was still clearly enjoying the novelty of filming in color and the opening shots are beautiful, with the red army uniforms standing out like blood on a handkerchief – a lavish, lingering spectacle, it is at odds with the rambling and melodramatic plot.

Under Capricorn saw Hitchcock returning in style to film at Elstree. He saw himself as the famous Hollywood producer and director returning home in triumph, marshalling his fine British cast around him; Michael Wilding, Margaret Leighton and Cecil Parker were topped off by two of the world's biggest stars – Ingrid Bergman and Joseph Cotten. He expected to present the resultant masterpiece to a grateful world. But that world had come to associate Hitchcock with a particular style of film, and none of the key elements which were his hallmarks were in evidence in *Under Capricorn*.

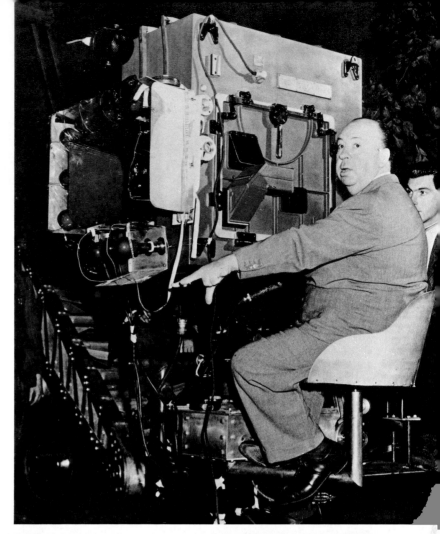

Right: *Hitchcock in his perennial uniform of suit and tie directing* Under Capricorn.
Below: *Michael Wilding on the set of the same film.*

While the film is set mainly in Hitchcock's safe, controllable studio world, the second unit shots of London at the beginning show what a battering Hitchcock's birthplace had taken during the war. The London of 1950 was a city still struggling with austerity and rationing, groaning under a Labour government which was trying to rebuild a country devastated by six years of war.

Stage Fright concerns Jonathan Cooper (Richard Todd), who tells his girlfriend Eve Gill (Jane Wyman) that the well-known actress Charlotte Inwood (Marlene Dietrich) came to his flat in a state of shock, confessing she had killed her husband and begging him to destroy her incriminating blood-stained dress before the police discover it. Cooper explains that the police saw him leave Charlotte's flat and now he is suspected of murder. He stays with Eve's father, the eccentric Commander Gill (Alastair Sim), while Eve enrols as Charlotte's maid in order to spy on her. At the film's conclusion, Todd is trapped in an empty theater and it is revealed that he killed Dietrich's husband in order to marry her.

Below: *Jane Wyman, the gullible heroine of* Stage Fright.

Above: *James Bridie, Scottish playwright who worked on* Under Capricorn *and* Stage Fright *(1950).*
Opposite: *The ever-glamorous Marlene Dietrich in* Stage Fright.

Hitchcock was too confident of his own abilities to take any real notice of the critics and he persevered with his next project, *Stage Fright* (1950), which again brought him back to work in London. For once, Hitchcock began believing his own publicity; when Selwyn Jepson's novel *Man Running* was published, Hitchcock remembered that 'several of the reviewers had mentioned that it might make a good Hitchcock picture. And I, like an idiot, believed them!' The novel was adapted by Alma, with additional dialogue provided by Scottish playwright James Bridie (who had also worked with Hume Cronyn on the ill-fated *Under Capricorn*). Installed at Elstree Hitchcock set to work with a magnificent cast of British players including Michael Wilding, Alistair Sim, Sybil Thorndike, Miles Malleson, André Morell, Irene Handl, Arthur Howard and Joyce Grenfell. Global appeal was ensured by the inclusion of Marlene Dietrich and Jane Wyman.

Hitchcock was keen to make a film with a stage background and 'the idea that the girl who dreams of becoming an actress will be led by circumstances to play a real life role, by posing as someone else in order to smoke out a criminal.' The theatrical background had a personal side, Hitchcock's only daughter Patricia was studying drama at RADA in London and appears in a small role in *Stage Fright*. For all his scathing comments on actors and the acting profession, Hitchcock was undeniably fascinated by the theatrical environment and was keen to immerse himself in it again, as he had done in *Murder* (1930). *Stage Fright* is steeped in this atmosphere, most notably in the scene of the theatrical garden party, which features every well-known British acting face he could lay his hands on.

Above: Stage Fright*'s theatrical garden party with the inimitable*
Alastair Sim *in white hat.*
Below: *The director on location in Gower Street, London.*

Todd was a relative newcomer to the screen and turned in a reliable performance as Cooper, although his greatest triumphs lay ahead in the 1950s with his stalwart roles in *Rob Roy – the Highland Rogue* (1953) and *The Dam Busters* (1954). Jane Wyman was recovering from being married to Ronald Reagan and had just scored two impressive performances in *The Lost Weekend* (1945) and her Oscar winning role in *Johnny Belinda* (1948). Dietrich was, incomparably, Dietrich, and Alastair Sim his own beloved self.

Marlene Dietrich lived up to her reputation as a true Star; Dior designed her gowns at a cost of £2000, her old friend Cole Porter duly wrote *The Laziest Gal In Town* for her to sing at the theatrical garden party and she delivered the film's best line, 'Detectives are only policemen with smaller feet!' Hitchcock caustically commented of her at the time, 'Marlene Dietrich is a true professional; a professional actress, a professional cameraman, and a professional dress designer!' But Hitchcock's real problem on set was with Jane Wyman, who had to appear dowdy and mousy as Dietrich's maid, which was fine until she saw the rushes and realized how ineffably glamorous Marlene appeared by comparison; she subsequently rushed off set at every available opportunity to be made more glamorous.

The major flaw of *Stage Fright* is the pivotal use of Todd's story, told in flashback, at the outset of the film, but which was

BCL 382

eventually shown to be a lie. The audience were thus more than usually, and perhaps unfairly, hoodwinked for the bulk of the film. The American critic Myron Meisel wrote: 'Movies do not lend themselves either to expressing the consciousness of individual characters or to lying; a concrete reality of images generally conveys too great a presumption of reliability, as Hitchcock discovered in his experiment with a prevaricating flashback in *Stage Fright*.' It was a device which unsettled the audience and which even Hitchcock later regretted: 'I did one thing in that picture that I never should have done; I put in a flashback that was a lie.' After all, the audience *has* to believe what the characters on screen are saying, it is the only relation with them, the audience must follow their thread otherwise they are lost – particularly when the character is such a reliable cove as Richard Todd! *Stage Fright* marked a pleasant diversion for Hitchcock but while its English stage background retains a certain period charm, it is indisputably a minor work.

Right: *Hitchcock outside RADA, where his daughter was studying during the filming of* Stage Fright.
Below: *The film's washed-out garden party recalls the umbrella murder in* Foreign Correspondent.

THE FOURTH
DECADE

Entering his fourth decade as a filmmaker, Alfred Hitchcock could bask in the knowledge that he had established himself as one of the major forces in world cinema. Thanks in no small part to his contribution, Hollywood had grown up, establishing the genre of *film noir* which Ephraim Katz described as 'the dark and gloomy underworld of crime and corruption, films whose heroes as well as villains are cynical, disillusioned and often insecure loners, inextricably bound to the past and unsure or apathetic about the future.' Key films of the genre included Hitchcock's own *Notorious* and *Spellbound*, as well as Fritz Lang's *The Woman in the Window* (1944), Billy Wilder's *Double Indemnity* (1944) and Tay Garnett's *The Postman Always Rings Twice* (1946) from the mid-1940s. It was into this shady underworld that Hitchcock plunged again in 1951, following the high jinks of *Stage Fright*, *Strangers on a Train* (1951) presented the darker side of the coin.

Hitchcock purchased the film rights to Patricia Highsmith's novel of the same name for a mere $2000 and commissioned Raymond Chandler to work on a screen treatment. On paper, it seemed like a marriage made in Heaven – Hitchcock, the supreme master of the suspense thriller, working with Chandler, creator of Philip Marlowe, the quintessential screen private eye, and author of some of the most cynical, witty and trenchant dialogue the private-eye genre has ever heard. But in practice it did not work out.

Right: *Alfred and Patricia Hitchcock during the filming of* Strangers on a Train *(1951), their second film together.*
Below: *Farley Granger and Robert Walker's first meeting on the train.*

Hitchcock said rather bluntly that Chandler's work was 'no good,' and an assistant of Ben Hecht's, Czenzi Ormonde, was brought in to help out. However the finished script was arrived at, it paid off when the film was released. After the disappointments of *Under Capricorn* and *Stage Fright*, critics hailed *Strangers on a Train* on its release as one of the 'thrillers of the decade' and welcomed Hitchcock's return to form.

The film is a perfect example of the exchange murder theory, the enticing possibility of committing a perfect crime. Two men meet by chance on a train with no link except that they both stand to benefit from the murder of someone close to them; what if they were to kill each other's victim, providing the suspect with a perfect alibi for what seem like two random crimes?

The plot of *Strangers on a Train* is a complex one, the exchange murder scenario goes ahead, except that one of the principals does not go through with his part of the bargain. Although the evil Bruno (Robert Walker) has already murdered Guy's wife, Guy (Farley Granger) refuses to murder Bruno's overbearing father, so Bruno tries to coerce him by threatening to plant a piece of incriminating evidence – Guy's lighter – at the scene of the crime. However he is crushed to death by a roundabout before he can incriminate Guy, who is cleared.

Top: *(l to r) Patricia Hitchcock, Farley Granger, Ruth Roman and Leo G Carroll from* Strangers on a Train.
Above: *Granger and his estranged wife (Laura Elliott), who is later murdered by psychopath Robert Walker.*

Above: *The perfect murder goes horribly wrong for Robert Walker at the conclusion of* Strangers on a Train.

Walker is chillingly effective as Bruno, one of Hitchcock's few authentic villains – notice the way he relishes bursting the child's balloon at the fairground prior to the murder, how mean can you get ! Sadly though, this was to be his penultimate film and he died in 1951. Granger appeared again as a weak, manipulated character whose objections to murder seem to owe more to cowardice than to moral scruples. Leo G Carroll makes a welcome, though unlikely, reappearance as Senator Morton, lending an air of dignity to the film's secondary characters.

The set-pieces of the film are stunning – the classic moment is near the film's finish. Having established Guy as a well-known tennis professional, Hitchcock obviously could not resist the temptation to show him playing. While Bruno is planting a piece of crucial evidence at the scene of the crime, the scene switches to a game of tennis which Guy is desperate to finish in order to thwart Walker's plans. Typically Hitchcock even manages to elicit sympathy for the clearly psychotic Bruno; when at one stage he drops Guy's lighter down a drain on his way to plant it and is frantically trying to retrieve it through the grating, the audience is with him all the way. Also notable is the murder of Guy's wife (Laura Elliott). It happens at night on a lonely island in the middle of a busy fairground; having enticed her away Bruno toys with her, flirting and lighting cigarettes, before slowly strangling her. Hitchcock brilliantly introduces new life to the scene by having it played out against the reflection of the girl's glasses.

Robert Walker's portrayal of a psychopath is stark and effective. A party game goes horribly awry when, lightheartedly demonstrating the technique of strangulation, he catches sight of Barbara Morton (Patricia Hitchcock) whose glasses remind him of the murdered woman and the hapless guest on whom he is demonstrating nearly dies. Another scene which lingers is the shot of the tennis crowd moving their heads in time with the volleys, with the exception of the sinister Bruno who sits staring straight ahead. He has become Guy's nemesis, shadowing him wherever he goes; he crops up as an unwanted party guest and solitary figure on the steps of the Capitol undermining Guy's whole future. *Rope* dealt with philosophic murder, *Strangers* deals with practical murder. Hitchcock manages to elevate the mundane into the extraordinary; a chance encounter on a train does not usually lead to the subject of murder being seriously discussed; it is to Hitchcock's credit that he not only makes this happen, but makes it seem entirely plausible.

For his 30th sound feature film *I Confess* (1952), Hitchcock turned to a 1902 play by Paul Anthelme, *Our Two Consciences*. Hitchcock's film deals with a Catholic priest, Father Logan (Montgomery Clift), who hears confession from his sexton Keller (Otto E Hasse) and learns that he has committed murder. Bound by the sanctity of the confessional, Logan cannot reveal his findings to the detective LaRue (Karl Malden) and finds himself suspected of the murder. Logan is brought to trial but although found not guilty by the jury, on leaving the courtroom he is attacked by an angry crowd. The killer's wife, knowing of Logan's innocence, rushes to protect him, but is murdered by her husband, who in turn is shot by the police. While he lies dying Keller once again confesses to Logan, this time in front of enough witnesses to clear Logan's name once and for all.

The film was advertised at the time with the grisly byline 'Crushed Lips Don't Talk!' Hitchcock was dissatisfied with the treatment, calling it 'heavy handed, lacking in humour and subtlety.' What is fascinating of course is the strength of the priest's inner conviction, how far can he be pushed before he will break the inviolability of the confessional? *I Confess* is remarkable for a Hitchcock film as we are told within the first five minutes who the murderer is, what his motives were and how he managed to evade capture.

Below: *A misleadingly passionate publicity still from* I Confess *(1952).*

Above: *Detective Karl Malden restrains Montgomery Clift as his innocence is revealed in* I Confess.

The theme of a wrongly indicted man unable to trust the police to clear him is familiar enough but, uniquely, in this film the accused's own beliefs stand in the way of his clearing his own name. Here we have the familiar fallibility of the police aided and abetted by the suffocating doctrine of the Roman Catholic church, contriving together, in the name of Good, to nearly destroy an innocent man who is willing to die for the crime of another rather than betray his own beliefs.

The film is striking for its deeply personal echoes of the Hitchcocks. The sanctity of the confessional obviously struck a chord with Hitchcock's Catholic upbringing, and the murderer's wife was called Alma. Hitchcock was eager to search out interesting locations in Quebec, which gives a new sense of freedom in contrast to the recent strict confinements imposed by *Lifeboat* and *Rope*. On paper *I Confess* seems like no more than a dissertation on the morality of the confessional, but in fact it is as rich in plot as any of Hitchcock's more secular works – there is murder, suspense, blackmail, betrayal and death.

The film is rich in religious imagery. In one shot the camera catches Father Logan walking tormented past a church, the camera placed high above one of the Stations of the Cross, as if making the point that Father Logan too is undertaking his own solitary journey to Calvary. The film's opening shot is an elliptically angled view of a looming church, darkly brooding and sinister. Clift's lonely inner struggle to sacrifice himself rather than his beliefs is contrasted with the killer's pathetic need to confess, as if by telling of his sin his guilt will be absolved. This central theme is frequently a problem for non-Catholics, who cannot understand how guilt can be cleared by the simple act of confession, and this is the flaw which Hitchcock felt the film retained: 'We Catholics know that a priest cannot disclose the secrets of the confessional, but the Protestants, the atheists,

Above: 'Killer priest' (played by Montgomery Clift) is witnessed leaving the scene of the crime in I Confess.

the agnostics, all say "Ridiculous! No man would remain silent and sacrifice his life for such a thing."' Father Logan's sacrifice and the difficulties of the audience are all the greater because Keller is such an unsympathetic figure, a German refugee who positively gloats over the murder, and revels in Clift's inability to tell the police and save himself. Perhaps because of this fundamental difference of perception, Hitchcock rarely allowed overt Catholicism to intrude on his films. He even once declined an audience with the Pope, commenting, 'What if the Holy Father disapproved of my movies? What if he said "Alfred, lay off the killing"?'

The flaws of the film however were not confined to the fallibility of the plot. Anne Baxter was miscast as Clift's former girlfriend and Hitchcock had problems communicating with Clift, who was then at the apogee of his career and steeped in the Method school of acting which was just manifesting itself in Hollywood, thanks largely to Marlon Brando's awesome performance in *A Streetcar Named Desire* (1951). After Brando, Clift and James Dean were the foremost exponents of the Method, which primarily meant that the actor got inside his character, and concentrated on motivation and background to deliver a fully rounded portrayal of the person, not just as the camera caught him for a specific scene, but where he had come from, where he was going, what impelled him to be there – the very antithesis of Hitchcock's methods. Clift's biographer, Robert LaGuardia, wrote that Hitchcock 'simply couldn't understand the fanatical intensity of a Monty. He complained constantly about "all that preparation" . . . Over and over, Hitch had to stop and explain to Monty why, at the end of a certain scene he had to look up at a church or suddenly turn around. He wasn't used to having to explain to his actors that he intended to edit in a shot of a clanging bell or some other such event.' The contrast between actor and director manifested itself early in the shooting, when the blue-eyed Clift insisted on wearing brown contact lenses because the script stated that Father Logan's eyes were brown. Hitchcock found this totally incomprehensible, not least because *I Confess* was in black-and-white.

Below: Flashback to Clift's stormy romance which continues to haunt him after he has taken his vows.

I Confess was shot on location in Quebec in under two months, but there was a hitch when the Catholic authorities saw George Tabori's original script and stopped all use of their churches in the city, because in the original draft Clift's character was found guilty. Rather than fight the Catholic fathers, Hitchcock instructed Tabori to alter his script. Tabori later recalled: 'I felt betrayed. I walked out in the middle of a story conference with the excuse of having to take a leak, went straight to the airport, to New York City, and never came back.' Unworried, Hitchcock simply commissioned William Archibald to alter the script to his satisfaction.

Clift had serious alcohol problems during the shooting of *I Confess* and his only ally on set was Karl Malden, who played the detective. Malden, an actor with a distinguished screen career, had just completed *Streetcar* with Brando, and Clift felt that he was sympathetic to his burning acting intensity. Anne Baxter was a Warners' contract player foisted on Hitchcock. She had proved her ability with an Oscar-winning performance in *The Razor's Edge* (1946) and as the conniving actress in *All About Eve* (1950) but for the role of Clift's former lover she was unsuitable. *I Confess* garnered only moderate reviews on its opening, and highlights Hitchcock's inconsistency. His career fluctuated unpredictably – he could effortlessly make a masterpiece like *Rope* and follow it with the dreary *Under Capricorn*, bounce back with the taut *Strangers on a Train* and follow that with the one-dimensional *I Confess*.

Above: *Rope*'s *New York skyline in the studio posed innumerable problems for Hitchcock on his first color film.*
Below: *1948 publicity poster for* Rope.

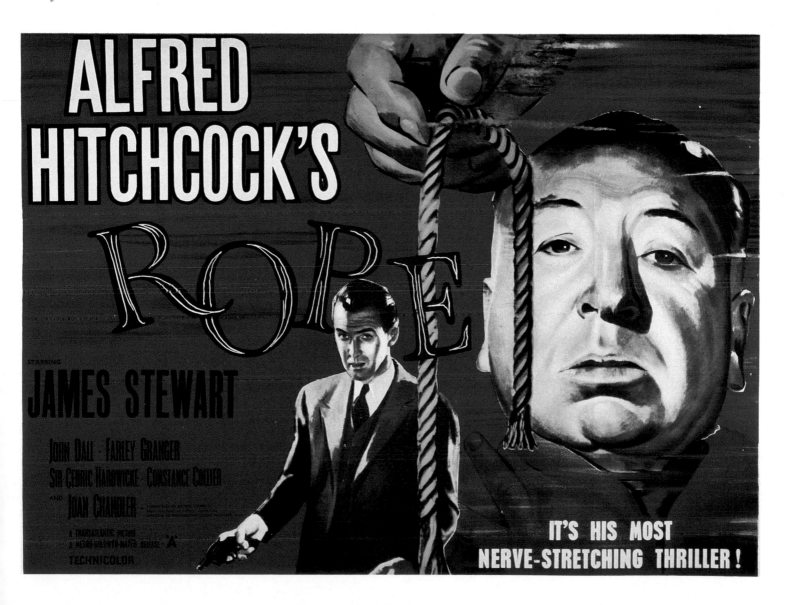

For his next project Hitchcock was attracted by Frederick Knott's play *Dial M For Murder* which had enjoyed successful London and Broadway runs. The wily Alexander Korda purchased the screen rights for a paltry £1000 from the author and then promptly sold them to Hitchcock – allegedly the following night over dinner – for £30,000.

Dial M For Murder (1953) is essentially a 'howdunnit.' Tony Wendice (Ray Milland), a retired tennis player, knows that his wife Margot (Grace Kelly) is having an affair with thriller writer Mark Halliday (Robert Cummings). Wendice coerces a seedy old Cambridge contemporary Lesgate (Anthony Dawson) into murdering her. But it is another 'perfect murder' which goes terribly wrong when Lesgate is killed by Margot during the struggle. Wendice realizes that he can still inherit Margot's £90,000 by making it look as though she cold-bloodedly killed Lesgate, not in self defense but because she was being blackmailed by him. He succeeds and Margot is sentenced to be hanged. But neither Mark nor Inspector Hubbard (John Williams) is convinced of Margot's guilt, and eventually they set an elaborate trap and catch Wendice redhanded just in time to save Margot's life. From the beginning the audience knows Milland is the guilty party, the question is – how long will it be before the police realize that?

The whole plot hinges on the whereabouts of the two keys to the Wendices' flat, one of which is used by Lesgate when he comes to murder Margot. *Dial M For Murder* is a straightforward murder yarn, with Hitchcock determined not to 'open up' the successful stage play. He retains its stagy elements by filming it virtually on one set, that of the Wendices' flat. The film stands or falls on Knott's plotting and dialogue (unusually, Hitchcock retained him to adapt his own play for the screen), and on a straightforward 'but Inspector, there's just one thing I don't understand . . .' type of melodrama. As such it is highly successful, although as the whole film centers around the availability of only two keys to the flat, one constantly wonders why Milland did not simply have half a dozen copies made. But such is Hitchcock's skill and experience at skimming over such incongruities that this does not spoil the enjoyment of the film.

After the dexterity of *Rope*, *Dial M* is an oddly flat Hitchcock film. It is not totally lacking in technical innovation, however, for as well as being made available as an 'ordinary' film, it was also shot as a 3-D feature. The 3-D technique was one of the weapons in Hollywood's arsenal to fight back at the encroaching television invasion. By the early 1950s in America television was breaking the cinema's stranglehold on entertainment and the moguls were clearly worried; Jack Warner, for example, refused to allow a television set to be depicted in any of his films! The cinema fought back with devices such as VistaVision and Cinerama, determined to emphasize the *big* screen appeal of cinema. 3-D was one of their main weapons, but prior to *Dial M* it had been used solely as a gimmick, on such forgotten films as *Bwana Devil* (1952) and *Hondo* (1954). Hitchcock was obviously attracted to the possibilities but felt its impact was likely to be short term. Even on a flat viewing of *Dial M* objects like bottles and lamps are placed prominently at the front of the shots and characters make flamboyant gestures with items such as scissors and keys to emphasize the extra dimension. The

Opposite: *Ray Milland making a pivotal phone call in* Dial M For Murder *(1953).*

clumsy spectacles required for viewing these films were ultimately too much trouble for audiences, and like so many other gimmicks tried by Hollywood 3-D soon disappeared, and *Dial M For Murder* stands as its single best example.

Hitchcock retained John Williams and the gaunt Anthony Dawson in their original stage roles; Ray Milland (who had won an Oscar in 1945 for his harrowing performance as an alcoholic in *The Lost Weekend* [1945]) was Tony Wendice, and turns in an urbane and calculating performance. Obviously relishing the dialogue, he remains supremely calm under pressure – at the moment of his arrest he blithely helps himself to a stiff drink and politely inquires if anyone wishes to join him.

But the real star of the film was Grace Kelly. Although he had not been unduly impressed by her earlier films, *Mogambo* (1953) and *High Noon* (1952), Hitchcock was fascinated by her icy beauty and 'potential for restraint.' From her very early scenes in *Dial M* his camera gently ravishes Kelly, who is dressed in beautiful gowns. At one point Hitchcock even acceded to her suggestion that she play the crucial murder scene in a nightdress rather than a dressing gown.

While filming *Dial M* the director and star were cordial. Kelly was respectful and Hitchcock, though infatuated, was as usual supremely controlled. Kelly's performance in the film is correct without being inspired and although Hitchcock revelled in her natural beauty she had yet to attain the glacial quality which later became the trademark of her onscreen persona.

The film's finest scene is very reminiscent of *Strangers on a Train*, when Milland coaxes Dawson into murdering his wife. There are other similarities too; like *Strangers* it is the seemingly chance encounter which leads to the plan for the perfect crime, and like Guy in the 1951 film, Tony Wendice is a professional tennis star. Wendice lures Lesgate to his flat by pretending that he wishes to buy his car. Gradually it emerges that Wendice and Lesgate were contemporaries at Cambridge, appearing together in a college photo which also features Hitchcock's sombre face. As Wendice's demands become more dangerous Lesgate fights shy, but Milland is teasing, insidious and manipulative and toys with Lesgate's character for some time before revealing that he has enough material to blackmail him. Wendice has made a hobby of following Lesgate after a chance sighting in a pub ('there were times I felt you belonged to me' he smoothly tells Lesgate), and it is then that the audience realizes how cool and deadly Wendice is. As the complexities of the plot are revealed and the perfect murder is unrolled, the fascination is whether Wendice will pull it off.

It is a brilliantly sustained scene: Wendice, chill and calculating, is completely in control of the situation, while Lesgate, at a complete disadvantage, is nervy and avaricious. Postwar London was full of characters like Lesgate, who had not enjoyed a particularly 'good war' and were desperate for money to keep up appearances. Perfectly at home as Inspector Hubbard, John Williams is calmly authoritative, exactly how cinema audiences expect Detective Inspectors to be – pipe smoking, rational and keen to get straight to the truth of the matter. Unusually for a Hitchcock policeman, Hubbard will not let the matter rest, even with Kelly found guilty and condemned to death. John Williams lent a calm authority to *The Paradine Case* and *To Catch a Thief* and went on to appear in a number of Hitchcock's television shows.

Dial M For Murder is straightforward entertainment,

ALFRED HITCHCOCK'S
dial M for Murder

PRESENTED BY
WARNER BROS. STARRING   NEW HITCHCOCK EXCITEMENT IN **WARNERCOLOR**

RAY MILLAND · GRACE KELLY · ROBERT CUMMINGS

JOHN WILLIAMS · WRITTEN BY FREDERICK KNOTT WHO WROTE THE SENSATIONAL STAGE SUCCESS · DIRECTED BY ALFRED HITCHCOCK · MUSIC COMPOSED AND CONDUCTED BY DIMITRI TIOMKIN

deliberately stagebound by Hitchcock, who saw his role as no more than filming the play in as effective a manner as possible. The only real diversion from the play is a slightly surreal 'trial' scene, where Grace Kelly is shown head and shoulders against a shifting colored background while the prosecution establishes her 'guilt,' and the judge is shown having the terrifying black cap placed on his head to deliver sentence. This scene, which seems so distant now, was at the time only too real – Ruth Ellis, the last woman to be hung in Britain, did not die until July 1955, two years after the film was released.

From the stagy London of *Dial M For Murder*, Hitchcock returned to contemporary America for his next film *Rear Window* (1954). But America was changing, and although Hitchcock was not the sort of filmmaker to directly concern himself with contemporary issues, the changing mores of American society helped place his films in context. During the early 1950s the United States had undergone a massive social transformation. In 1954, while Hitchcock was shooting *Rear Window*, a young truck driver called Elvis Presley was sweating in the Sun Studios in Memphis, creating a hybrid of Rhythm & Blues and Country & Western which was the birth of rock 'n' roll. James Dean was just slouching into Hollywood. The benzedrine prose of Jack Kerouac's *On the Road* had fired the Beat Generation. The age of the teenager had at last arrived.

Hanging over it all though, was the specter of the atom bomb. When it became apparent just what those scientists at

Above: *Poster for Hitchcock's only 3-D film,* Dial M for Murder. *The clumsy spectacles required for watching these films were too much trouble for audiences, and the gimmick was soon dropped by Hollywood.*

Los Alamos had been working on when Hitchcock was filming *Notorious*, America developed a terrifying hostility and postwar isolationism. Fearful that the Russians would invent their own bomb and rocked by unsettling reports of US spy rings (Klaus Fuchs, Alger Hiss and the Rosenbergs being the most notable), America turned inward and began looking for Reds Under the Bed. The blustering, bullying, egotistical Senator Joe McCarthy began building a political career out of terror tactics – his invidious, mostly fictitious 'list of Communist subversives' supposedly hard at work in high government circles spawned the House Committee on Un-American Activities, which deliberately sought out and victimized sympathizers in the early 1950s.

The family unit lived in the shadow of the bomb, with its own fallout shelters, and was not going out to the movies much. Even though the drive-ins retained some of their appeal, television had taken over as the prime source of entertainment. With all these seismographic changes going on outside, Hitchcock kept to the security of the studio where in a controlled environment he was at liberty to create his own world. The finest example of his ability to do just that came with *Rear Window*.

'The best directors are those who become emotionally involved with what they're doing' Grace Kelly told her biographer Steven Englund. There can be little doubt that while filming *Dial M For Murder* Hitchcock had fallen in love with his leading lady. Hitchcock was only too keen to renew their professional relationship at the earliest opportunity and it was this covert passion which resulted in his finest film, *Rear Window*.

The film is ultimately Hitchcock's most disturbing work. Long after the shock of *Psycho* is forgotten and the cosy suspense of *The 39 Steps* has gone, the questions of morality and involvement, of voyeurism and responsibility raised by *Rear Window* linger on. It is James Stewart's finest performance; it shows Grace Kelly as Hitchcock wanted her seen; and technically it remains an outstanding contribution to the language of cinema. But Hitchcock's true genius is that he never allows his unquestioned technical superiority to overshadow or hinder the narrative thrust. We never forget what a fine story *Rear Window* is, even while we sit in awe of the look of the film. When the film was revived in London in 1983 many critics felt that despite being 30 years old it was the film of the year.

Above: *Ray Milland doing some quick thinking after Grace Kelly has thwarted his plans,* Dial M For Murder.
Below: *Grace Kelly grappling for her life with Anthony Dawson in* Dial M For Murder.

Stewart plays LB Jeffries, a globe-trotting magazine photographer, confined to his apartment by a broken leg during a sweltering New York heatwave. Bored and easily distracted, he finds his attention increasingly drawn to the apartment of Lars Thorwald (Raymond Burr) opposite. Gradually Jeffries comes to believe that Thorwald has murdered his wife and disposed of her remains. He confides his theories to his daily nurse Stella (Thelma Ritter), a detective friend Doyle (Wendell Corey) and the elegant Lisa Fremont (Grace Kelly) with whom Jeffries is enjoying a sporadic romance. All of them are initially skeptical, accusing him of being nothing but a peeping tom. The pieces slowly fall together and Thorwald is indeed revealed to be a murderer, trapping and nearly killing Jeffries in his own apartment, before the police manage to rescue him after a cliff-hanging climax.

The plot was drawn from a story by the thriller writer Cornell Woolrich, who was not happy with the screen treatment, and his dislike kept the film out of circulation for many years due to a lengthy legal wrangle. Hitchcock went on to enjoy a fruitful creative relationship with scriptwriter John Michael Hayes, a writer in his mid-30s whose first screen credit was *Rear Window*. He worked on Hitchcock's next two films and later scripted the screen versions of *Peyton Place* and *The Carpetbaggers*.

Hayes had the opportunity to see at first hand how Hitchcock's obsession with Kelly manifested itself. The director decided on Kelly for the role of Lisa and told Hayes to tailor the dialogue for her, even before the actress herself was asked. When offered the role of Lisa, Grace Kelly was considering the role in *On the Waterfront*, which Eva Marie Saint eventually took and won an Oscar for. Ironically it was to Eva Marie Saint that Hitchcock later turned when in 1959 Grace Kelly declined to star in *North by Northwest*. Hayes told Steven Englund: 'He would have used Grace in the next 10 pictures he made. I would say that all the actresses he cast subsequently were attempts to retrieve the image and feeling that Hitch carried around so reverentially about Grace . . . I was entranced by her. I hadn't expected to be, but I was. I couldn't get over the difference between her personal animation and, if I may say so, her sexuality . . . There was an alive, vital girl underneath that demure, quiet façade; she had an inner life aching to be expressed, but she wasn't drawing on it.' Hayes was keen to highlight both aspects of the Kelly character in his script, to which Hitchcock enthusiastically agreed.

Opposite: *James Stewart and Grace Kelly in a publicity shot for* Rear Window *(1954)*.
Below: *One of the views from Stewart's rear window.*

Above: *Hitchcock surveys the spectacular set of* Rear Window.

For once, Hitchcock's concern for the performance of an actress almost interfered with his general overview of the film. At one point where Kelly was simply required to plant a kiss on Stewart's forehead, Hitchcock insisted on shooting the scene 27 times! He instructed costume designer Edith Head that Kelly must look like a piece of Dresden china throughout, a challenge that the redoubtable Miss Head relished.

Understandably, the finished film reflects Hitchcock's obsession with the actress, but it is to Stewart's credit that he manages to make the character of Jeffries so vital despite his immobility. There is a famous anecdote Hitchcock loved to recite about the audience reaction to Stewart's view of the world from his apartment window: 'Let's take a close up of Stewart looking out of the window at a little dog that's being lowered in a basket. Back to Stewart who has a kindly smile. But if in place of the little dog, you show a half naked girl exercising in front of her open window, and you go back to a smiling Stewart again, this time he's seen as a dirty old man!' It is that power of montage, of cutting, which Hitchcock holds sacred; all the actors had to do was react and he would create the performance when editing. The technique itself was not new, its possibilities had been shown years before by the Russian silent directors Hitchcock had admired in his youth. Lev Kuleshove and his pupil Vsevolod Pudovkin experimented by taking a single expressionless close-up of an actor and intercutting this one shot with three different scenes: a plate of soup, a coffin containing a woman's body and a little girl playing with a toy. In his book *Film Technique and Film Acting* Pudovkin wrote: 'The public raved about the acting of the artist. They pointed out the heavy pensiveness of his mood over the forgotten soup, were touched and moved by

the deep sorrow with which he looked on the dead woman and admired the light happy smile with which he surveyed the girl at play. But we knew that in all three cases the face was exactly the same!'

The supremacy of *Rear Window* lies of course in its gripping narrative but the film also stands as a testimony to Hitchcock's ability as a director – the architect of film structure, the craftsman whose camera roves, intrudes, caresses, creates and destroys. Virtually all the audience sees is the view from photographer Jeffries' New York apartment – *Rear Window* is just that! Yet Jeffries is only one tiny constituent part of the block, of the neighborhood, of the city. It is as if by chance that Hitchcock decides to concentrate on Jeffries, when there are so many other memorable tales to be told even in that one apartment block. It is by the same sort of chance that Jeffries' attention is particularly drawn to the apartment of an undiscovered murderer. Even his enforced restriction to one window offers an extraordinarily wide choice of subjects for study, many of them just as interesting and mysterious: the shapely Miss Torso, the pitiful Miss Lonelyhearts, the struggling songwriter, the pathetic childless couple or the passionate honeymooners whose marriage quickly degenerates into bickering and mundaneness. Hitchcock certainly gave some thought to the random potentiality of the film, he said to Truffaut of the songwriter: 'I wanted to show how a popular song is composed by gradually developing it through the film, until, in the final scene, it is played on a recording with a full orchestral accompaniment. Well it didn't quite work out the way I wanted it to and I was quite disappointed.' Interestingly, the song heard in the party scene is *Mona Lisa* which was a hit for Conway Twitty in 1959.

It is the pathetic Miss Lonelyhearts (Judith Evelyn) who engages most sympathy. She is seen at her heartbreaking dinner for one, then making her way into the big world outside her apartment – visiting the bar across the street, and later rebuffing an all-too-ardent suitor in her apartment. So involved do Jeffries, Stella and Lisa become in the excitement of Thorwald's 'real' murder that they seem at times more like accomplices to the crime than detectives. In the meantime, they all but ignore Miss Lonelyhearts' suicide attempt. Their prurience has almost obliterated their ability to do anything about a real death taking place in front of their eyes. Benign

Below: *Stewart tenaciously explains his murder theories; Kelly allures to no avail.*

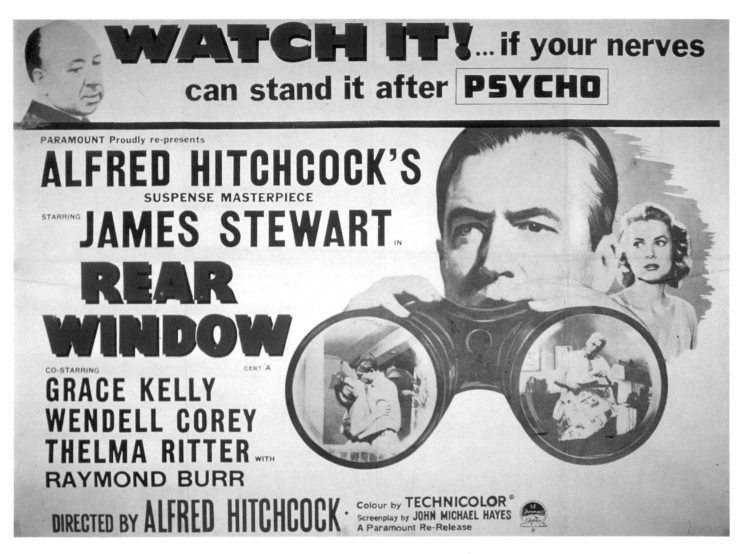

intervention would be easy but again they cast themselves in the role of titillated observers and accomplices. It is the trio's indifference to the fate of Miss Lonelyhearts which almost causes her death and touchingly portrays the essential isolation and aching sense of loneliness in a big city.

It is Thelma Ritter, giving an inestimable performance, who supplies the film's message: 'We've become a race of peeping toms. What people ought to do is get outside of their own house and look in for a change.' (In impact and effect, the only comparable film to *Rear Window* is Michael Powell's dark masterpiece *Peeping Tom* [1960], in which a young photographer kills his victims and photographs them in their death throes.) Hitchcock responded to criticism of the film's prurience by retorting 'What's so terrible about being a voyeur? Sure, he's a snooper, but aren't we all? I'll bet you that nine out of 10 people, if they see a woman undressing for bed, or even a man pottering around his room, will stay by the window and look.' That same voyeurism extends into today's television soap operas, 'slices of life' in which the audience can eavesdrop on the traumas and triumphs of ordinary people without any fear of being caught. On the film's reissue in 1983 the *Sunday Express* wrote: 'is not this like so many of us today, taking gratification from, say, our TV screens at the expense of wholeheartedly enjoying the challenge and reward to be found in our own lives?' A timely reminder of Thelma Ritter's perspicacious sentiments in the film.

Jeffries' curiosity in *Rear Window* begins as a harmless diversion; imprisoned in his plaster cast he longs for the wilds of Kashmir or Shanghai. This passing interest develops

Top: *Poster for* Rear Window; *the film was reissued in the 1960s.*
Above: *Raymond Burr – the 'is he, isn't he?' murderer of* Rear Window.

Above: James Stewart focusing his attention on the sinister events in the opposite apartment.

through prurience to obsession and into direct action. It is after Detective Doyle seems to have proved halfway through the film that Thorwald could not have murdered his wife that Jeffries reflects to Lisa: 'I wonder if it's ethical to watch a man with binoculars and a long-focus lens . . .?' To which Lisa replies: 'I'm not very good on rear-window ethics . . . We're sitting here unhappy because a man didn't murder his wife. We're two of the most frightening ghouls I know!' Their disappointment at Thorwald's apparent innocence reveals again the cracks in their relationship. We can only speculate as to how Jeffries and Lisa met and were attracted to each other, maybe the truth is that opposites do attract. Eventually they compromise happily and in the film's final scene marriage beckons.

There is so much to appreciate in *Rear Window*. Even Hitchcock's cameo as a clock repairman seems significant: a man who can repair a complex piece of machinery making it a perfect device to knoll the passing of time. The script is darkly bitter with Stella savoring lines like: 'Where do you suppose he cut her up? The bathtub's the only place, to wash away the blood. He'd better get that trunk out of the way before it starts to leak!' Jeffries starts a romantic evening with the seductive Lisa by asking 'Just how would you start to cut up a human body?' There is the tantalizing idea that all of this is merely a figment of Jeffries' overfertile imagination; what has he imagined, where does speculation end and fact take over? As in *Suspicion* the audience is not sure until the end of the film whether they are witnessing a wife murderer or merely a suspicious imagination working overtime.

Rear Window hangs together like a mathematical puzzle, which once taken apart can never be perfectly reassembled, but sublimely knitted together by Hitchcock it stands as his timeless masterpiece. One can imagine his joy at seeing the finished set, like FW Murnau who came to Hollywood in the 1920s to film *Sunrise* (1927) and, incredulous at the scale and authenticity of the set, spent a whole day walking and crawling all over it! There is also the technical challenge for Hitchcock, to show only what can be seen from Jeffries' apartment. This helps the audience identify even more strongly with the character, sharing in his frustration at being so confined and his impotence at being unable to help Lisa when she is trapped in Thorwald's apartment. There is also the magnificent death-defying excitement of the climax. As Jeffries, trapped with Thorwald in his apartment, is forced toward the window ledge, his fingers frantically grasp the ledge but, forced by Thorwald, Jeffries slips down. Rather than have the standard shot of Stewart's fingers slipping and cutting to the body falling a few feet to the ground, Hitchcock places his camera above Stewart's body and in one shot we see him fall 30 feet to the patio. It is with such bravado that Hitchcock captures the hearts of even the nontechnical.

There is no doubt that in *Rear Window* Hitchcock portrays his own dream heroine. His camera ravishes Kelly from her first appearance; her head fills the screen, her voice is silkily seductive as she leans forward to kiss Stewart. Every gown, every movement is a hymn to Kelly's perfection; even the caustic Stella has nothing but praise for Lisa Fremont – only Jeffries is unmoved by her perfection. *Rear Window* is one of Hitchcock's most overtly sexual films. Lisa's overnight bag leaves little to the imagination, neither does her parading in a negligee inquiring of Jeffries 'Like what you see?' The idea that an unmarried girl could openly stay overnight in the apartment of a bachelor must have taken some swallowing in 1954. Even after the Kinsey Report on Sexuality (published in 1948) Hollywood's attitude to sex remained puritanical.

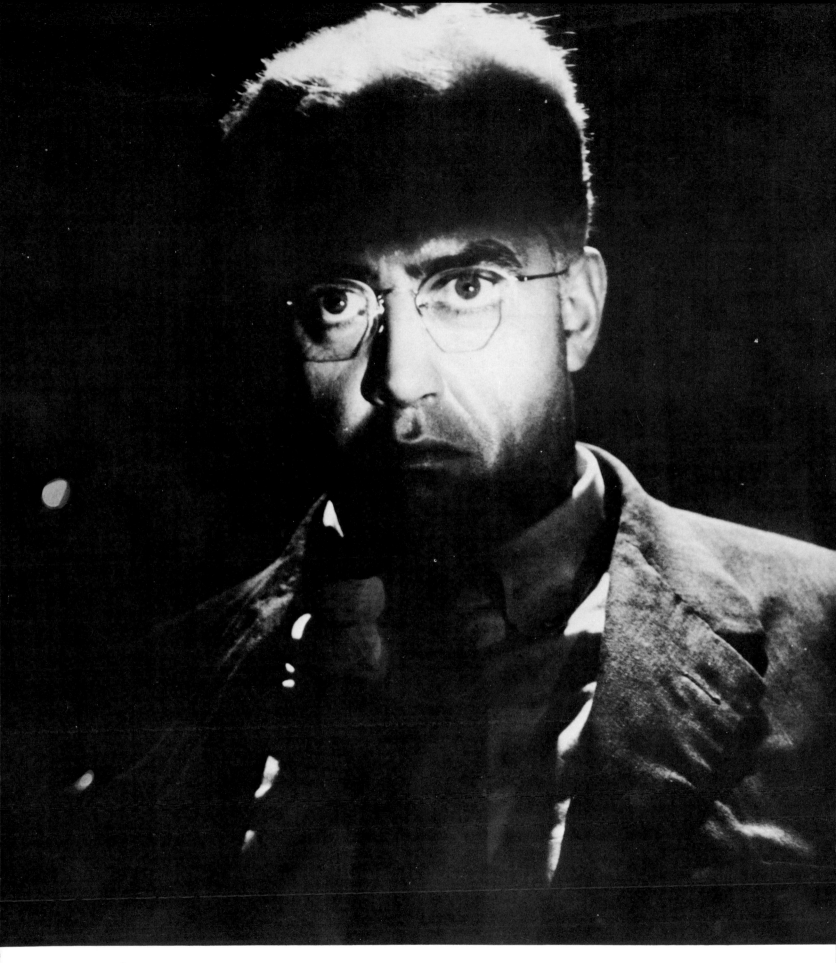

At the conclusion of *Rear Window* we see a selection of contented images. Hitchcock, having zoomed into the apartment block, now pans out, waves his director's wand and with the ease which fiction allows, grants everyone a happy ending. Miss Lonelyhearts has found companionship with the songwriter; the childless couple have a new puppy; Miss Torso's unlikely soldier boyfriend has returned home; and Lisa is seen inelegantly clad in combat gear grimacing through a

Above: Sinister Raymond Burr pays a late-night visit to Stewart's apartment.

travel book, before surreptitiously switching to *Harper's Bazaar*, while Jeffries contentedly dozes. Thorwald has been caught and brought to justice, life in the apartment block resumes its meandering course. Order has been restored.

Below: *Cary Grant, apparently out of danger in* North by Northwest *(1959)*.
Inset: *Posters for* The Man Who Knew Too Much *(1956) and* Vertigo *(1958)*.

THE
MASTER OF SUSPENSE

After the brooding and claustrophobic intensity of *Rear Window*, Hitchcock sought relief in the South of France with a lightweight piece called *To Catch a Thief* (1955). The story concerns former Resistance hero and retired jewel thief John Robie (Cary Grant) who is concerned that a thief working in his style is leading police to believe that he is still active. With the help of Frances Stevens (Grace Kelly), Robie sets out to catch a thief, which he duly does. He becomes engaged to Frances but is less than enthusiastic to learn that mother will be coming too. Frances' mother (Jessie Royce Landis) is a draconian figure recalling the overbearing Mrs van Hopper of *Rebecca*, particularly in the scene where she extinguishes her cigarette in the yolk of a fried egg.

For Hitchcock of course the opportunity to work with Grace Kelly on their third film together in under two years was welcome. As with Cary Grant, Hitchcock seemed capable of tapping Kelly's hidden depths. Steven Englund wrote: 'Infatuated with Grace's reserve and beauty, Hitchcock recognized that the key to unlocking her cinematic potential was to get Grace to stop leaning on 'acting' techniques alone, and to draw instead upon her emotions in rendering a part . . . Over the course of three films Hitchcock succeeded in drawing forth Grace's gift for romancing the camera with her beauty.' But Englund cautioned: 'In *To Catch a Thief*, Grace

Above: *Hitchcock celebrating his birthday with Cary Grant and Grace Kelly on the set of* To Catch a Thief *(1955).*

sparkled with real luster, but she could go no further with Hitchcock. The two best roles he gave her, were, in the final analysis, unsympathetic, two-dimensional manipulators of men!' It was, of course, during the filming of *To Catch a Thief* that Kelly first met Prince Rainier, whom she subsequently married, leaving Hollywood and Alfred Hitchcock behind forever. It was almost as if Hitchcock intended the film to be a farewell present. Edith Head recalled: 'It was a costume designer's dream . . . The most expensive set up I've ever done. Hitchcock told me he wanted her to look like a princess. She did!' Certainly in the film's lavish costume ball, Grace Kelly had never looked lovelier.Following his marriage to Betsy Drake, Grant had not made a film in 15 months, and had no intention of returning to the screen. Only Hitchcock could, and did, persuade him. Even with the parallel attractions of working with Kelly and the exotic Riviera locations, Cary Grant promptly finished work at six o'clock each night and was disturbed by Hitchcock's overt presence on set: 'It seemed like the only passionate words of love I ever spoke to her were with Hitchcock staring in my face!' As already noted, Hitchcock would tap hidden depths in Grant's screen persona, because as he himself recognized: 'I've always taken the average man and got him involved in the extraordinary. That's how a man like Cary Grant has been cast, because they represent someone with whom the audience will identify rather than worry about.' This curious empathy was barely noticeable in *To Catch a Thief*, but reached its apogee in *North by Northwest*.

John Michael Hayes' script bubbles along but never really boils over. There is a nicely ambiguous and justly famous picnic scene with Kelly coyly cooing: 'I've never caught a jewel thief before. It's so stimulating. Do you want a leg or breast?' To which Cary Grant responds 'You make the choice.' 'Tell me, how long has it been?' 'Since what?' 'Since you were in America!' It is always a pleasure to see two such professionals perform, one only wishes that for their only film together a more memorable vehicle than *To Catch a Thief* could have been found. For despite the scenic Riviera loca-

Left and opposite: *Two aspects of life on the Riviera in* To Catch a Thief.

11511-67

Top: *Retired jewel thief Carry Grant back in action in* To Catch a Thief.
Above: *Cary Grant in* To Catch a Thief, *his third Hitchcock film.*
Above right: To Catch a Thief *was Grace Kelly's last film for Hitchcock; during the filming she met her future husband, Prince Rainier.*

tion work, Robert Burks' Oscar-winning photography and the comic interplay between Grant and Kelly, *To Catch a Thief* never really catches fire. On its release, *Variety* remarked: 'Billed as a comedy/mystery it stacks up as a drawn out pretentious piece that seldom hits the comedy level.'

To Catch a Thief seemed, even at the time, a curiously anachronistic film; a glittering, opulent jewel, recalling the standards and traditions of 'old' Hollywood. With 'kitchen sink' dramas like *Marty* (1955) and *The Man with the Golden*

Arm (1956), and 'youth' movies like *East of Eden* (1955) and *Rebel without a Cause* (1955) all the rage, it was natural actors like James Dean, Ernest Borgnine and Marlon Brando who were the new stars. Even by halfway through the turbulent 1950s, stars like Grant and Kelly seemed like throwbacks to a former era of glamour and escapism.

A film like *To Catch a Thief* serves as a reminder that Hitchcock is a great populist filmmaker along the lines of the great John Ford, that he is capable of producing pieces of enjoyable froth such as *To Catch a Thief* or *Dial M for Murder*, as well as enduring masterpieces like *Rope* and *Rear Window* which add to the vocabulary of cinema, enhancing its possibilities and expanding its parameters. Hitchcock's distinction was that he consistently attained that difficult balance between critical and popular acclaim. It was in the mid-1950s that Hitchcock was championed by a group of French film directors including Claude Chabrol, François Truffaut and Louis Malle: *les enfants terribles* who later went on to become influential filmmakers, at the forefront of the French 'new wave.' Like the 1970s Movie Brats, these cineasts lived and breathed film and revered Hitchcock's work, putting him in such eminent critical company as Orson Welles, Sergei Eisenstein and DW Griffith. Hitchcock was flattered and more than a little embarrassed by such attention. For him, filmmaking was a job; he was punctilious on set but never took his work home with him. He was like the production-line directors of Hollywood's Golden Age such as Michael Curtiz and Billy Wilder, whose films were their jobs – although on more than one occasion those 'jobs' became enduring cinematic masterpieces like *Casablanca* (1942) and *Sunset Boulevard* (1950). Even into the 1980s the Movie Brats never forgot those whose work had inspired them; Martin Scorsese and Francis Ford Coppola revered Michael Powell's work, John Milius greatly appreciated Howard Hawks and Steven Spielberg was a passionate advocate of Hitchcock.

It was the French critics of the 1950s who first coined the *auteur* theory of filmmaking. This says that the director is literally the 'author' of a film, that his influence extends far beyond simply setting up a shot and instructing the cameraman what to shoot. The *auteur* shapes the whole film, gives it substance and depth. The earnest enthusiasm of the young French critics thereby discounted the very real contributions made by scriptwriters, composers, cameramen, actors, set designers – all the hundreds of individuals whose co-operative effort goes into creating a full-length feature film. There are convincing examples of the *auteur* at work: Selznick was virtually solely responsible for *Gone With The Wind*, writing, part-directing and casting the film as well as producing it. Orson Welles responded exuberantly to the challenge of filmmaking by tackling every facet of it head-on; no one can take away from Welles his supreme achievement – *Citizen Kane*. And yes, the *auteur* theory can justifiably be applied to Hitchcock.

From the 1930s on there was a series of distinguished, easily recognizable genre films which have the stamp of an 'Alfred Hitchcock film.' It should be remembered that Hitchcock started at the bottom of the film industry and slowly worked his way up (there was no lower post than that of caption writer) and Hitchcock went on to immerse himself in all aspects of the creative process which together make a film. Hitchcock's practical understanding of the film trade in all its aspects ensured that he had an intelligent contribution to make on a practical level. But to categorically state that *Rear*

Above: *Cary Grant strolling in the Riviera sunshine.*

Window is exclusively the work of Hitchcock ignores John Michael Hayes' magnificent script; the tortured brilliance of *I Confess* owes as much to the intensity of Montgomery Clift's performance as it does to Hitchcock's direction; Lyle Wheeler's art direction for *Rebecca* created the Manderley which millions remember with affection; and Launder and Gilliat's inventive screenplay for *The Lady Vanishes* has elevated the film to a cult classic. This is without even considering the contributions of Peter Lorre, Robert Donat, Dame May Whitty, Charles Laughton, Joan Fontaine, George Sanders and Joseph Cotten, among a cast of thousands!

Undeniably Alfred Hitchcock left his stamp more distinctively on his films than many of his contemporaries and successors. William Goldman amusingly and witheringly dismisses the concept of the *auteur* in his compelling book *Adventures in the Screen Trade*: 'Hitchcock became, along with Cecil B. de Mille, one of the two most famous directors in the business ... Just what the auteurists were looking for. Famous, but ignored critically. With a personal vision. Perfect! ... Once an auteurist surrenders himself to an idol, for reasons passing understanding, said auteurist flies in the face of one of life's basic truths: people can have good days, and people can have bad days.' In fairness, Hitchcock did have more good days than bad.

Below: *Hitchcock proudly posing with a photo of him being presented to the Queen.*

Even Hitchcock's most devoted fans must have scratched their collective head at his choice of next film. *The Trouble with Harry* (1956) was originally a novel by English writer Jack Trevor Story. Hitchcock was in familiar company. Scriptwriter John Michael Hayes and cinematographer Robert Burks were working on their third consecutive Hitchcock film. Surprisingly, the director remembered the film as one of his own favorites. A 'newcomer' to the repertory company was composer Bernard Herrmann, who had scored *Citizen Kane* as his first film assignment. He went on to work with Hitchcock on a further seven films.

The Trouble with Harry concerns a rather troublesome corpse, which keeps turning up in a tiny Vermont town. A young boy discovers the corpse and runs to tell his mother. Crusty old seadog Albert Wiles (Edmund Gwenn) stumbles across it and assumes he must have killed it accidentally while rabbit shooting. The boy's mother, Jennifer (Shirley Maclaine), gleefully recognizes it as her former husband Harry, and wonders if the blow she gave him with a milk bottle was fatal. The town doctor literally trips over it. Painter Sam Marlowe (John Forsythe) sketches it and then helps Wiles bury it, disinter it and bury it again. Spinster Miss Gravely (Mildred Natwick) confides that she killed Harry with her shoe after he tried to molest her. Eventually, even the slow-minded deputy (Royal Dano) realizes something is amiss and eventually it is discovered that Harry actually died from natural causes. Which just leaves time for Jennifer and Sam, and Miss Gravely and Wiles, to announce their engagements before life resumes its normal, sedate course in upstate Vermont.

Above: *Mr and Mrs Hitchcock off to scout new locations in 1956.*

Below: *Forsythe and Gwenn in* The Trouble with Harry *(1956).*

It's a whimsical, slight film, charming in a subdued way; spread over 96 minutes the charm begins to pall. The gamine Maclaine makes an entrancing film debut and Gwenn relishes his role as the sea captain, who turns out only to have been an East River tugboat captain! Gwenn, a Hollywood stalwart from the silent days, was 75 when he made *Harry*, and 16 years earlier he had appeared in an uncharacteristically sinister role as the failed assassin who tries to push Joel McCrea from the top of Westminster Cathedral in *Foreign Correspondent*. John Forsythe, now more familiar as the gray-haired patriarch of the Carrington clan in TV's *Dynasty*, makes an engaging artist as Sammy Marlowe.

The Trouble with Harry is the nearest Hitchcock came to making a pure comedy. The lovely, lingering opening shots of Vermont at the height of its autumnal beauty set the scene for the whimsy that is to follow. The small town is endearingly Capraesque, even more folksy and friendly than Santa Rosa in *Shadow of a Doubt*. Edmund Gwenn is such a lovable old rogue, one wonders whether his physical similarity to Hitchcock is mere coincidence, or if that is why he was chosen – particularly in the scene where he is dozing in a chair. The element of fancifulness is nowhere more apparent than in the scene where the struggling artist is visited by a conveniently passing millionaire who decides to buy all his paintings and asks what he wants for them. He simply asks for the items his friends desire most in the world: a hunting rifle, strawberries and 'a cash register, chromium plated that rings a bell' for the storekeeper.

Hitchcock said that one line characterized the appeal of the film for him. As Albert Wiles struggles along pulling the

Above: *Maclaine (left) in* The Trouble with Harry.

corpse at the beginning of the film, he is chanced upon by the timid Miss Gravely who gently inquires, 'What seems to be the trouble captain?' For Hitchcock, the lasting charm of *Harry* is that 'I took melodrama out of the pitch-black night and brought it out into the sunshine ... These contrasts establish a counterpoint; they elevate the commonplace in life to a higher level.' There are a number of enchanting scenes which suggest what Hitchcock was aiming to achieve: Shirley Maclaine, telling John Forsythe of her singularly undistinguished wedding night with Harry, goes on to discuss his death and the quality of the lemonade; Maclaine's precocious son, 'What do you call that rabbit, Arnie?' 'Dead!'; and Wiles's lascivious comment on Miss Gravely, 'A well preserved woman ... and preserves are there to be opened someday!' But too much of the film is concerned with stagy conversations on death and mortality. The film's cuteness soon becomes cloying, especially when it is realized that it is nothing more than 'a comedy about a corpse' as the adverts had it, that no element of danger or threat, no change of pace will occur. Just who murdered Harry is open to question until the very end; at one time it seems that, as in *Murder on the Orient Express*, everyone may be guilty.

The lightness and airiness of the film is established with its opening shot of a beautiful, white-boarded church, nestling in the verdant New England countryside – quite unlike the brooding Gothic church which opens *I Confess*, but setting the atmosphere in a very similar way. The characters are cute to the point of biliousness; the artist is temperamental, zany and brilliant; the old sea dog is predictably full of adventures up the Orinoco; the spinster serves 'blueberry muffins, coffee

Above: *Poster from one of Hitchcock's own favorite films.*

and a little elderberry wine'; there is unlimited credit at the village store; the village doctor is an amiable eccentric who stumbles around reciting poetry at the dead of night; the six-year-old Arnie delivers the sort of lines which suggest a team of scriptwriters slaving away in his nursery; no one drinks anything stronger than lemonade; and the only car to pass through the village contains a philanthropic millionaire. It makes the world of Frank Capra seem about as cosy as that of Sam Peckinpah!

The real trouble with Harry is that it is not a very funny comedy or a particularly effective thriller. While Harry hovers ghost-like over the whole proceedings, one simply starts wishing that his murderer would be swiftly discovered, so that the corpse can find sanctuary in the local morgue. In general, the film was poorly received in America, but it had a strangely warm reception in Britain, with the *New Statesman* commenting: 'The whole film is enchanting and for the first time in his

Below: *John Forsythe and Shirley Maclaine, the young romantic leads in* The Trouble with Harry.
Right: *The trouble with having a quiet tea for two . . .*

career – in his own mellow fall – Hitchcock reveals a touch of poetry.'

Hitchcock's reputation by the mid-1950s was substantial; he was the only film director whose name and face were as well known to the public as any star's. Hitchcock had actively cultivated this cult of celebrity; from the economic necessity of appearing in his own early films to help 'swell the ranks' had grown his enormously popular cameo appearances. Hitchcock always made himself available for interview and was guaranteed to produce a lugubrious anecdote or dry aphorism, ensuring that every interviewer went home happily with good copy. However, despite the huge popular following if *The Trouble with Harry* had been representative of Hitchcock's work in the mid-1950s his reputation may have been in serious danger. But being the wily businessman that he was, Hitchcock had seen the possibilities of television and as usual rose to the challenge. As one of the most public faces of cinema ever, Hitchcock was a natural for television, and with 260 episodes of *Alfred Hitchcock Presents* (and a further 93 of *The Alfred Hitchcock Hour*), which ran between 1955 and 1961, Hitchcock had conquered another medium.

Television was accurately called a medium in the 1950s because, as one wag wrote, 'It is neither well nor badly done!' But Hitchcock's shows lent a certain dignity and style to the airwaves. There were around 260 half-hour episodes of *Alfred Hitchcock Presents* aired between 1955 and 1961, of which Hitchcock only actually directed around 15. *The Alfred Hitchcock Hour* ran between 1962 and 1964, but Hitchcock directed only one episode, *I Saw The Whole Thing* in 1962.

The format never varied, Gounod's *Funeral March of a Marionette* played against Hitchcock's pencil drawing of his own portly profile which ushered in the all-too-recognizable figure of the genial host. Hitchcock's lugubrious introductions were memorable – Hitchcock seen in a torture chamber demonstrating the rack; Hitchcock in a cinema box office talking about Pay TV; Hitchcock tied to railway lines advising viewers about plane travel; Hitchcock talking about the family unit he aimed for on set, as an arc lamp crashes on his vacant chair . . .! Hitchcock's accent remained remarkably English after all his years in America. His accent, unlike Cary Grant's, remained totally English, classless and rather sinister. Never one to avoid the limelight, these little cameos showed Hitchcock revelling in his reputation as 'The Master Of Suspense.'

The material for *Alfred Hitchcock Presents* was drawn from a wide range and included adaptations of stories by such authors as Dorothy L Sayers, John Mortimer, Ray Bradbury, Nicholas Monsarrat, Saki and A A Milne. Writers who worked on the shows included regular Hitchcock contributors such as Robert Bloch (author of *Psycho*) and Cornell Woolrich, author of *Rear Window*. Other familiar names were Philip Roth and Roald Dahl. The series also gave valuable experience to new directors like Robert Altman and Arthur Hiller. Established names such as Raymond Massey, Claude Rains, Bette Davis, Joseph Cotten and Fay Wray were regularly featured, and rising new stars like Steve McQueen, Richard Chamberlain, Robert Duvall, James Coburn and Charles Bronson received early breaks on the shows.

Hitchcock's own personal favorite from the *Alfred Hitchcock Presents* series was *Lamb to the Slaughter* which Hitchcock directed from a Roald Dahl short story. It concerns a frustrated wife who murders her husband with a frozen leg of lamb she has been saving for Sunday lunch. The police arrive and are baffled by the murder, figuring that if only they could

Above: *Hitchcock introducing one of his early TV shows.*

find the murder weapon, they would have found the murderer. Enter bereaved wife with a snack for the mystified and hungry policemen – as they eat their lamb, they muse, 'If *only* we could find that weapon. For all we know, it's right under our noses!'

All the half hour shows were deftly filmed, with a neat twist at the end. For example *Incident in a Small Jail* directed by Norman Lloyd (who had appeared in *Saboteur* and *Spellbound*) is about a travelling salesman who is wrongly imprisoned, only to be revealed at the end as a psychopath. *Road Hog* was a pacy story about a callous driver who causes the death of a farmer's son, only to suffer at his hands; the show paired Raymond Massey and Richard Chamberlain years before their success together in *Dr Kildare*. *The Diamond Necklace* was an elegant tale with Claude Rains as a mild-mannered jewelry store clerk who carries on the family tradition by stealing a priceless necklace.

The shows were particularly successful on American TV, partly because of the sheer quantity of material needed to fill their demanding program schedules. The networks were delighted with the quality and quantity of *Alfred Hitchcock Presents* and the shows were regularly rerun for many years. There was no doubt that Hitchcock's own introductions aided the shows' popularity, particularly when he was irreverent about the shows' sponsors – tantamount to heresy on American television.

Above and Left: *More moments from the Master in the* Alfred Hitchcock Presents . . . *TV shows, which ran for seven years.*

In 1985 four of the best shows were remade with new casts but sticking to the original 1950s screenplays. They, were aired on American television and released in Britain on video, which prompted Simon Hoggart's laconic comment in *Punch*: 'The most famous living Englishman is probably Alfred Hitchcock. The best of his late night TV thrillers have been filmed again, but NBC has tacked on the old introductions by Hitch himself, cunningly tinted for colour sets, so that he looks even more deathly than he presumably does under the ground!'

One of the most interesting was *Man From The South*, originally featuring Peter Lorre and Steve McQueen, remade with John Huston as the maniac who collects little fingers from his victims' left hand for a bet! The casting displayed an irony Hitchcock would have appreciated, as it boasted cameo appearances from Tippi Hedren and Kim Novak.

The television series, however, was to remain a sideline for Hitchcock; for him movies were his life blood. To the surprise of many he began in 1956 to remake his own 1934 film *The Man Who Knew Too Much*. Hitchcock is on record as vastly preferring the later version, citing among other reasons the subtle humor, Bernard Herrmann's orchestration, the placing of the shots and James Stewart's performance. It is difficult to imagine just how Hitchcock could prefer the remake. While the 1934 version may be occasionally stilted, its brevity and wit put it on a par with *The Lady Vanishes* while the 1956 version is flaccid and overlong. The technical improvements do not compensate for the overall dreariness of the later film, which at times seems like a clumsy parody of Hitchcock; the fight in the taxidermist's shop, for example, is designed as a set-piece *divertissement* but it comes across as contrived, irrelevant and humorless. The scene in an Arabian restaurant is a tedious and parochial view of how 'funny' foreign food is, and how difficult a tall man like James Stewart finds it to sit on a native divan. Bernard Miles is seriously miscast as the villain and the final shoot-out at the Albert Hall, while allowing Hitchcock to revel in the symmetry of the venue, lacks the suspense to hold the audience. The supposed climax at the embassy is simply a tedious coda, which appears to have been tacked on as an afterthought.

While the majority of Hitchcock films happily allow the audience to suspend their disbelief, blissfully unconcerned with the actual mechanics of the MacGuffin, the 1956 *The Man Who Knew Too Much* contains more jarring notes than even the most credulous audience can easily accept. When

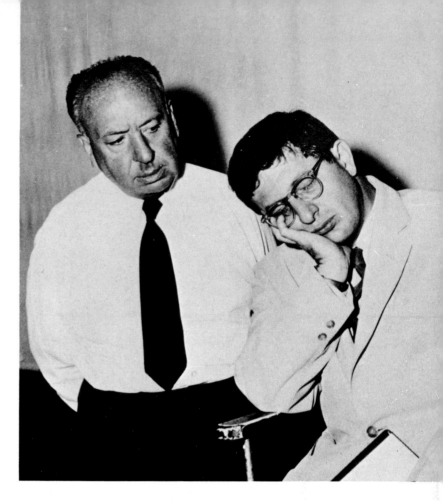

Above: *Hitchcock and sleeping partner while filming* Vertigo *(1958).*
Below: *Hitchcock on location in Marrakesh, for once having dispensed with a jacket.*

Above: *The Marrakesh market murder that sets the ball rolling in the 1956 remake of* The Man Who Knew Too Much.
Below: *Stewart follows up one of several red herrings in the same film.*

Stewart is trapped in the chapel, why doesn't he just break a window and escape, rather than practicing for his role in *Vertigo* by making an elaborate exit via the church tower? Could anyone honestly hear young Hank whistling on another floor in the vast embassy while Doris Day is in full voice at the piano? And isn't it fortunate that with a capacity of 6000 and a rather elaborate system of boxes and gangways, Stewart is able to spot Doris Day within 10 seconds of arriving at the Albert Hall?

The remake is stiff and stilted, spread over an interminable two hours. Despite strenuous efforts at assimilation, Day seems resolutely out of place in a Hitchcock film, only too swiftly seizing the opportunity to burst into song. (*Que Sera Sera* won the Oscar for Best Song in 1956 and reached No 2 in the US charts in the same year.) Doris Day and James Stewart epitomize the middle-class American family; responsible and loving parents, they glow with postwar pride in US achievements – in fact they are rather too good to sustain any interest. Their package holiday through Europe and North Africa is the old 'if it's Tuesday, it must be Marrakesh' syndrome. Even the location work in Marrakesh has the glossy and unreal look of a travel film – it is only toward the end of the bazaar scene, after Brenard has been stabbed and lies dying in Stewart's arms with his minstrel

Above: *Dying secret agent ensures that innocent James Stewart becomes the man who knows too much.*

make-up coming off on Stewart's hands, that any real impact is achieved. When Stewart is coshed in the chapel, it is a throwback to the overacting employed in silent films: the cosh descends on his head, his face is seen in close up, eyes rolling, and the room spins before him.

The climax at the Albert Hall, where Hitchcock allows the crucial foiling of the assassination to be played without any dialogue, is effective. The audience knows what Stewart is saying to the disbelieving policemen and dialogue is therefore redundant. But on the whole, the film is populated by totally unsympathetic characters who are also unbelievable. Bernard Miles and Brenda de Banzie – fine performers in their own right – are unsuited to their villainous roles. The showbiz friends of Doris Day are clichéd characters, crying 'darling' at every opportunity and drinking oceans of cocktails, but for all that are not in the least amusing. The London police are more than usually incompetent. Too many scenes are prolonged; Stewart and Day's arrival at Heathrow, and their interview with the police in which they refuse to cooperate are totally lifeless. Quite why Hitchcock chose to remake *The Man Who Knew Too Much* is a mystery; on the evidence of this film it is fortunate that this was the only example of him returning to something which was handled entirely adequately in the first place.

From the exotic locations of Marrakesh and the brightly colored frippery of *The Man Who Knew Too Much*, Hitchcock returned to the dark reality of grimy New York streets for the somber, documentary style *The Wrong Man* (1957) – his first black and white film since *I Confess*, five years before. Hitchcock's attention had been drawn to a magazine article about Manny Balestrero, a jazz musician wrongly accused and imprisoned as an armed robber. Hitchcock was fascinated by the dramatic possibilities the story posed and the opportunity to film a true story which had all the characteristics of his films of the previous 30 years.

To ensure absolute authenticity Hitchcock filmed every event in the story at the actual location, and kept his cameo to a shadowy prologue – in the style of his TV introductions – thus emphasizing that what follows is the truth, the whole truth and nothing but the truth. It is terrifyingly apparent that truth is at once stranger and more disturbing than fiction. The audience identification with Manny is intense: just try thinking what *you* were doing on a certain night, at a certain time, some months ago. Were there any witnesses? Can you provide a plausible alibi when positive identification, again and again, says you were somewhere else?

Henry Fonda in sadly his only Hitchcock film is superb as Manny. Fonda was never an actor to rely on histrionics or

trickery, his screen persona was a testament to the traditional American values. His very presence in a film was a force for good, which is why his only really villainous role, in Sergio Leone's *Once Upon a Time in the West*, was so dramatically effective. Whether he was Mr Lincoln in *Young Mr Lincoln* (1939), the earnest Tom Joad in *The Grapes of Wrath* (1940), or the voice of conscience in *Twelve Angry Men* (1957), Fonda epitomized the very best kind of man – moral, determined to see wrongs righted and totally incorruptible. Fonda was always a solid, reliable character, the champion of the underdog who will not be browbeaten or kowtow, but will hit a lick for what is right in the land of the brave and the home of the free.

It is because Henry Fonda played Manny Balestrero that his unjust imprisonment strikes such a responsive chord with audiences even today. Manny is a loving husband and father, trusting and reliable, when he finds himself plunged into this waking nightmare. His terror and disbelief are only too credible. As the inexorable wheels of justice grind on and Manny tries to prove his innocence, the audience wonders, as in so many Hitchcock films, when the truth will out, or, as this is real life, *if* the truth will out. *The Wrong Man* is one of Hitchcock's most frightening films, because it happened just as he shows it, because it is something every member of the audience dreads – being plunged into the midst of a Kafkaesque nightmare from which there is no escape.

The film blandly but chillingly depicts the due processes of the law – the formal arrest, the fingerprinting (when he stares at his inky fingers, Fonda recalls James Stewart in Hitchcock's previous film, staring at the make-up on his fingers in the bazaar), the imprisonment. When Fonda is handcuffed there is none of the joky camaraderie of Donat and Carroll in *The 39 Steps*; when those cuffs click, his liberty is taken away and his life can never be the same again.

Perhaps the most touching of the many memorable scenes in the film is when Fonda, arriving home one evening, is seized by the police on his doorstep only one footstep away from his family. Fonda stares uncomprehendingly at his accusers and guards; as the car speeds him away on the start of his nightmare journey, he turns and sees his wife preparing dinner in their kitchen, blithely unaware of the maddening spiral into which she is to be plunged. Indeed, it is Vera Miles' madness which gives the film its real poignancy, for even when Fonda is eventually found to be innocent, his poor wife

Opposite: *The wrong man is handcuffed.*
Below: *Fonda on trial in* The Wrong Man *(1957).*

Above: *Henry Fonda and Vera Miles in publicity shot for the grimly documentary style* The Wrong Man.

is still locked in her own sad world of paranoia. It is the nameless, faceless, Kafkaesque 'they' who will ensure Fonda's guilt, they who will smash any alibi, they who are determined to destroy the couple. Fonda's heartfelt, accusatory 'You realize what you've done to my wife?' as he faces the real criminal touches the heart.

The Wrong Man is a corrosive film, burrowing to the very heart of the American Dream, a film which, while never forsaking its authentic New York roots, uncomfortably pre-empts Orson Welles' film of Kafka's *The Trial* five years later. It is the sheer weight of evidence against Fonda which topples him. All the witnesses are convinced of his guilt – the three ladies in the insurance office who first bring him to the attention of the police, several small storekeepers, all are in agreement. How can the word of independent witnesses be doubted? It is on their evidence that the legal system is based. It is no surprise that Colin McArthur felt: 'the film which perhaps best conveys the underlying unease of 50s America is *The Wrong Man* . . . slowly and deliberately, the judicial process locks him into his role, his family disintegrates under the experience and his wife retreats into madness.'

The Wrong Man remains a remarkably modern looking film; Fonda's performance is that of a timeless man in the street, and the windswept streets of New York could be those of *Taxi Driver* 20 years later (a feeling enhanced by Bernard Herrmann's brilliant, jazzy scores of both films). Hitchcock obviously responded to the 'fact is stronger than fiction' element of the story; telling Truffaut with relish of the real criminal's words when apprehended: 'The thief, thoroughly scared, began to whine "Let me go. My wife and kids are waiting for me." I loved that line; it's the sort of thing you wouldn't dream of writing into a scenario . . . You simply wouldn't dare use it.' Hitchcock also revealed that he enjoyed the 'ironic coincidence' of the thief being caught as Fonda was praying for help, although he denied that it touched any deep set religious beliefs of his own. Hitchcock appreciated the opening of the film because of 'my own fear of the police.' Pushing 60, Hitchcock still remembered the time his father had him 'imprisoned' as a child!

The Hitchcock phenomenon swept on from the low-key documentary *Wrong Man* of 1957 to the psychedelic para-psychology of *Vertigo* (1958). Like Henry Fonda, James Stewart personified middle American reliability and trust, but in this, his last film for Hitchcock, he is portrayed as a querulous, questioning and ultimately unsympathetic character. This was the film which forever placed Hitchcock as the critics' favorite. His previous films had received courteous treatment, even when the critics quibbled about some of his motivation or plot choices, but only the French *auteur* theorists had elevated him to a critical and intellectual zenith. *Vertigo* now seems a sop to Hitchcock's intellectual disciples; in it he makes a return to the amateur psychology of *Spellbound*, although *Vertigo* as a film has much more in its favor.

James Stewart is Scottie Ferguson, a former policeman who was forced to retire because of his fear of heights. Scottie is asked by an old friend Gavin Elster (Tom Helmore) to shadow his wife Madeleine (Kim Novak) because of her suicidal tendencies. Scottie does so, falls gradually in love with Madeleine and saves her from drowning, but he is unable to climb up to save her again when she jumps from a church tower. He enters a rest home and, encouraged by his steadfast, besotted girlfriend Midge (Barbara Bel Geddes), slowly returns to normal. Years later he sees a secretary called Judy who looks strikingly similar to the late Madeleine. Stewart gradually works his way into the girl's confidence and begins to re-create her in the exact image of Madeleine, dyeing Judy's hair, making her dress as Madeleine did and so on. Gradually it becomes apparent that Judy *is* Madeleine and has been all along. She was actually Elster's mistress but the woman who plunged from the church tower really was his wife; Scottie's services had only been enlisted to ensure a

witness to the 'suicide.' Scottie eventually forces Judy to confess this by making her, and himself, go to the top of the same church tower – thus finally overcoming his fear of heights. In a tragic accident Judy, who Scottie still loves, tumbles, and falls to her death.

The ending is certainly Hitchcock's most effective ever. Just as it becomes clear what has actually happened, a nun appears – looking like a sinister vampire bat – and causes Judy to tumble while Stewart stares helplessly down. The climax is kept till the very last second and displays Hitchcock brilliantly sustaining suspense to the very end. That said, *Vertigo* is an uncomfortable film. The first part, detailing Scottie's growing obsession with Madeleine, is touching and fascinating as he unravels *her* obsession with the long-dead 'mad' Carlotta Valdes. But once Madeleine is 'dead,' the film plunges uncomfortably into the dark waters of psychology and exposition. The film's second half also reveals a darker, more sinister and thoroughly unpleasant side of Scottie's character; whereas before, we feel for Scottie because of his illness and the loss of the only woman he has ever loved, when his dark determination to turn Judy into Madeleine becomes apparent, we are completely alienated. Watching the film with a modern audience, it is possible to *feel* the hackles rising as Scottie orders Judy into gowns of his choosing, changes her hair until it suits him, so that she becomes a completely subservient creature, only existing as a product of his desire.

Stewart begins the film as his usual sympathetic self, scoffing at Elster's talk of psychiatry, psychology and re-incarnation! Bluff, amiable Stewart does not hold with any of that hocus-pocus. This is why the transformation from the reliable Scottie to the manipulative Svengali is all the more startling and why Stewart's performance is exemplary. Gradually we discern a darker side to his character, a Doctor Frankenstein constructing his dream, pursuing his lust, desire and vanity, oblivious to the feelings of others. Hitchcock retained a great fondness for Stewart, he once told Grace Kelly: 'Jimmy and I have a lot in common. He too, is a painstaking craftsman. Critics concentrate solely on his boyish grin and halting delivery and ignore his superb acting ability . . . Just watch the way he moves his hands and the rest of his body. Pay close attention to the eyes – a real professional.' This is Hitchcock's ultimate accolade to a performer – 'a true professional.' The enthusiasm ran both ways. Stewart commented: 'I have made four movies with Hitch. He had a way of bringing out the best in you . . . These days, we toss the word genius around entirely too much, but he *was* a genius in the picture business. He had a quality all his own that I don't think will ever be found in a director again.' Hitchcock certainly responded to Stewart's style and wrought three superb performances from him in *Rope, Rear Window* and *Vertigo*.

For the role of Madeleine/Judy, Hitchcock obviously had Grace Kelly in mind. One can see her svelte blonde beauty in the first half of the film but we can only speculate as to her proficiency in the second half. Following her touching performance in *The Wrong Man*, Hitchcock was keen to cast Vera Miles, but she became pregnant immediately prior to shooting. Finally, Kim Novak was cast – hot from *The Man with the Golden Arm* (1956) and *Picnic* (1956). She is surprisingly good in *Vertigo*, lending an ethereality to her role as Madeleine and

Left: Hitchcock's brilliant screen realization of James Stewart's fear of heights in Vertigo *(1958).*

Above: *Publicity shot for* Vertigo *which shows James Stewart and both characters played by Kim Novak.*
Right: *Stewart in an early scene from* Vertigo, *an episode which results in his phobia.*

sultry blowsiness to Judy. She responds well to Stewart's obsessive remodelling of her in the second half, and is undeniably sexy in the scene where she relaxes in Stewart's apartment wearing his dressing gown, after he has rescued her from drowning. Director Richard Quine summed up Novak's onscreen sensuality by saying she had 'the proverbial quality of the lady in the parlor and the whore in the bedroom.' Hitchcock however was unhappy with the choice of actress and less than responsive to the star's demands on the script and for costumes for the film. One example of the ambivalent relationship is Novak questioning (like Montgomery Clift) her character's motivation for a particular scene. 'Kim,' responded Hitchcock from behind the camera, 'it's only a movie!' (That apocryphal line, however, has been applied to virtually every star who ever appeared in a Hitchcock film!) Hitchcock lets his camera lovingly linger on Madeleine's first entrance into Ernie's Restaurant; his camera scans the wealthy diners, and inexorably zeroes in on her as she appears to glide in her beautiful evening dress, serene, stately and irresistible.

Vertigo was adapted from a novel by two French writers, Boileau and Narcejac, who, it is strongly rumored, wrote it specifically for Hitch to film. Saul Bass totally revolutionized the credit sequence in the mid-1950s; pre-Bass it was simply an opportunity to list the participants in the making of a

motion picture, but after his electrifying examples on *Around the World in 80 Days* (1956) and *Vertigo*, credits came into their own. It was John Ferren who designed the 'trip' sequence following Madeleine's death; Scottie's dream drills into his head and he undergoes a series of colorful, frightening plunges into his own psyche.

Vertigo is irrevocably remembered as a Hitchcock title, but has led to a popular misconception. Medically, vertigo is a form of giddiness, while the correct name for an actual fear of heights is acrophobia. Undeniably, though, *Vertigo* is a better title than 'Acrophobia'!

From the very first opening credit Hitchcock threw himself wholeheartedly into *Vertigo*. He revelled in the San Francisco locations, thoroughly welcoming the opportunity to film in one of the most beautiful American cities, which John Huston had used as the background for his directorial debut with *The Maltese Falcon* (1941). The streets of San Francisco are probably best known on screen from the action-packed chase scene in *Bullitt* (1968), filmed 10 years after Hitchcock shot

Below: *The chilling climax to* Vertigo. *Stewart conquers his fear of heights but loses his true love.*

IPS-7

Vertigo there. Hitchcock returned to the city briefly, for *The Birds* (1963) and for location work on *Family Plot* (1976), which was to be his last film. In *Vertigo* Hitchcock made full use of the architecture San Francisco had to offer. When Scottie tracks Madeleine down to the McKittrick Hotel, a dark, gloomy Gothic pile perched on the side of a hill, we can see the forerunner of the Bates Mansion in *Psycho*. At the tourist village, Hitchcock makes great use of the height of the church tower, and following Madeleine's suicide we see figures scuttling far below, like dots on an Escher landscape. Madeleine's other attempted suicide takes place by San Francisco's most famous landmark, the Golden Gate Bridge. To show James Stewart conquering his fear of heights Hitchcock ingeniously constructed a short staircase for the star to climb, then built a miniature of the winding staircase leading to the top of the tower, dollying and zooming his camera to create the feeling of phobia. The cliff-hanging climax of *Vertigo* recalls that of *Rear Window*, and is reminiscent of a similar scene which brought Michael Powell's eerie *Black Narcissus* (1947) to its tragic end. In the end, *Vertigo* is greater than the sum of its parts, but only just.

Vertigo stops one step short of necrophilia and that is perhaps what Hitchcock intended; trying to resurrect Grace Kelly for his own benefit when he knew she was far, far away, a princess now, with only her celluloid images left behind to remind the fans of what had been. Film is a permanent reminder of what was; it is also proof of how the director can create an image to his own ends. Is it too fanciful to see Stewart's Scottie, desiring to re-create that which he so dearly missed, as an extension of Hitchcock's own fantasy?

Hitchcock's next project was a collaboration with screenwriter Ernest Lehman, who had just written the acerbic *Sweet Smell of Success* (1957) which gave Burt Lancaster and Tony Curtis the best roles of their respective careers. Hitchcock and Lehman worked together on an adaptation of Hammond Innes' successful novel, *The Wreck of the Mary Deare*. This was based on the legend of the *Marie Celeste*, a classic seafaring yarn about a deserted ship found serenely sailing in the middle of the ocean, with the hot meals uneaten, the lifeboats unused, but no sign of passengers or crew! Hitchcock was very attracted to the idea but dropped the project because he felt that there was so much mystery at the outset that 'the rest of the story never quite lives up to the beginning.' *The Wreck of the Mary Deare* was in fact made into a worthy film in 1959, with an Eric Ambler adaptation of the Innes novel and Gary Cooper giving a memorable performance; but Hitchcock was quite right about the ending.

Hitchcock found Lehman an ideal collaborator and together they went on to fashion a delightful soufflé which became *North by Northwest* (1959). Hitchcock had one particular scene in mind when they began writing: the hero hiding in Abraham Lincoln's nostril on Mount Rushmore, and so for a while the film had the tantalizing working title of 'The Man in Lincoln's Nose'! It then briefly became 'In a Northerly Direction' before finally taking its cue from Hamlet's speech on his madness: 'I am but mad north-north-west; when the wind is southerly, I know a hawk from a handsaw.'

Even as Hitchcock and Lehman worked on the script it became apparent that it was to be highly literate and diverting, based on events with only the flimsiest connection with reality. Hitchcock saw virtually the whole film as a MacGuffin, 'the emptiest, the most non-existent and the

Above: *Cary Grant has one too many for the road in* North by Northwest *(1959)*.
Right: *Ernest Lehman, who brilliantly collaborated with Hitchcock on the original script of the film.*

most absurd!' The film's 136 minutes are spent in trying to track down a man called George Kaplan – the man who never was. Hitchcock and his many devotees regard *North by Northwest* as a synthesis of all his work, the apogee of his American period; indeed, the film's elegance and wit make a strong claim for this position. For while others may scratch their heads at the psychology of *Vertigo*, admire the technical expertise of *Rope*, appreciate the parochialism of *Shadow of a Doubt* and marvel at the dark genius of *Rear Window*, the sheer ineffable charm of *North by Northwest* is unbeatable.

Hitchcock and Lehman relished the prospect of making the script as complex as possible. They involve the hero in as many strands of a Gordian knot as the 136-minute film could bear. This is Alfred Hitchcock's longest film, for he believed that the length of a film 'should be directly related to the endurance of the human bladder.' Any synopsis of the plot makes for complex reading but in essence Cary Grant plays a suave advertising executive called Roger Thornhill, who is mistakenly identified by a mysterious group of spies as a secret agent called Kaplan. Pursued by the spies, Thornhill cannot go to the police, of course, but encounters Eve Kendall (Eva Marie Saint) who seems keen to help him, then betrays him, then ends up marrying him. On the run, Thornhill is pursued by the epicene villain, Philip Vandamm (James Mason), and his henchmen through all sorts of un-likely locations – the United Nations building, a crowded

Above: *Just when he thought it was safe to go back in the wheatfields . . .
Cary Grant in* North by Northwest.

auction room, Mount Rushmore, even an empty field where
he is pursued by a crop-dusting plane. In the end, Eve is
revealed to be an undercover agent, and she and Thornhill
are married and retire to a quiet life together.

Cary Grant worked with Hitchcock for the last time in this
film, and while his performance lacks the sustained intensity
of *Suspicion* or the callousness of *Notorious*, it is as Thornhill
that he is perhaps best remembered. Geoffrey Wansell in his
biography of Grant wrote: 'Hitchcock was determined to
make the centerpiece of the film the character that Cary
Grant had created over the years. The plot he and Lehman
had in mind depended on the audience identifying totally
with Grant as a man to whom terrible things happen, but who
nevertheless still seems never to lose control.' The scriptwriters piled complexity onto complexity with maniacal zeal,
much to the bewilderment of Grant, who complained halfway
through shooting: 'It's a terrible script, and I still can't make
head or tail of it!' Equally baffling is the choice of Jessie Royce
Landis as Grant's mother; she was, in fact, exactly the same
age as him!

Cary Grant was keen to have Sophia Loren playing Eve.
Hitchcock was hoping that his beloved Grace Kelly could be
lured back to the screen. In the event though the talented Eva
Marie Saint took the role, and held it with colors flying,
portraying a devious and enigmatic character. James Mason
stepped perfectly into the role of the villainous Vandamm. He
had already hewn a reputation as a sensual, sinister performer
in such films as *The Wicked Lady* (1945) and *The Seventh Veil*
(1945). As Vandamm he was a villain in the grand Hitchcock

tradition – cool, elegant and deadly, he was a worthy successor to Claude Rains, John Dall and Robert Walker.

In his autobiography Mason is particularly revealing about
Hitchcock's working methods with actors, confirming what
many already suspected. For Hitchcock, the fun of making a
film was in the preparation, writing the script, the logistics of
setting the film up, the preproduction. The actual filming was
a chore, a tedious process dutifully undertaken, so that the
rest of the world could see the film which had been running in
his head for months. Hitchcock was so certain of the infalli-
bility of his vision that a rumor often ran around his sets
(Mason certainly heard it during *North by Northwest*) that
once Hitchcock had received the OK from the sound and
lighting men, he ordered the cameras to roll and without
waiting to watch the scene enacted strolled off to the next set
up. Hitchcock told director Tony Richardson: 'The fun of
making a film is in the imagination of what I'm going to do.
The shooting is just an anticlimax!' In 1970, Hitchcock
continued the theme with Ken Ferguson: 'As far as I'm
concerned, the film has been made on paper, that's the most
important and fascinating stage . . . I wish I didn't have to go
into a studio. When you go onto a soundstage, that's when the
headaches really start!'

'Headaches,' of course, come largely from actors. Hitchcock simply saw the performers in his films as a part of the
overall process. The cinema-going public may be lured into
cinemas by the attraction of star names, and Hitchcock never
failed to appreciate the box-office potential of stars, but
during filming those stars were there to play a role which
Hitchcock had conceived, they were only acting out what the
script demanded. Having said that, many of the actors with
whom Hitchcock worked over the years had nothing but
praise for his skill in helping shape a performance. Where
Hitchcock and actors collided head-on was over the Method,
and in *North by Northwest*, there was an acolyte of that
discipline in the shape of Martin Landau, who played
Mason's henchman. He had attended the Actors' Studio in
New York for three years during the early 1950s and while
there had struck up an intense friendship with the young
James Dean. Landau confided to Mason that he had worked
out his role for a certain scene: 'There is a very clear
progression for me in the course of this scene, and step by
step I have planned exactly what I must do with it.' Arriving
on set, Hitchcock asked his secretary which set up they were
starting with, and dictated to his cast and crew exactly what to
do. Mason recalled: 'And so it was throughout the sequence.
The order of lining up the camera set ups was dictated by
Hitchcock's private set of logistics and took no account
whatever of Landau's carefully worked out progression!'
Mason understood better than most the central contradiction
in Hitchcock's relationship with actors: '(He) was a man who
asked for and expected no help from anyone other than the
technical aides with whom he set down the blueprints,
meticulously prepared, well in advance of the shooting stage.
The principal aide was his writer, and to greater and lesser
degrees, his cameraman, his editor and his art director. But it
is bad luck that an increasing number of actors feel that they
have to be "creative" and that it is their right and duty to make
"choices" which affect the staging of sequences and even the
text. For the likes of them, Hitch had no use . . . He had cast
them because their records had shown that they were capable
of playing the roles which had been unambiguously delin-
eated in his script.'

Above: *Eva Marie Saint 'kills' Cary Grant in* North by Northwest *as the stony faces of four US Presidents look on.*
Right: *Poster for the highly enjoyable* North by Northwest.

It is perhaps ironic that such cold calculation can make such a diverting piece of screen entertainment as *North by Northwest*. But it is because Hitchcock is so calculating that the overall effect of his films is so polished. *North by Northwest* is home to one of Hitchcock's best-remembered set pieces – Grant being chased by a crop-dusting plane. Summoned to a remote location (the innocent sounding 'Prairie Stop, Highway 41'), the ever-urbane Grant stands alone in the middle of a vast Midwest wheatfield. The audience breathes a sigh of relief, following Grant's recent hair-raising escapades, at least he is not in any danger here! Enter the plane, which immediately threatens like a demonic gnat. It is a masterly touch of Hitchcock's to place Grant at risk in such a seemingly innocuous location. The suggestion of menace is first introduced by a farmer boarding the bus, 'That's funny, that plane's dustin' crops where there ain't no crops!' So what is the plane doing? Surely there can be no danger? Danger is in dark alleys late at night; danger is the sound of persistent footsteps following our hero; it is dark and sinister, not light and open.

Total reliance on the MacGuffin factor makes *North by Northwest* a compelling entertainment, a cheerful inversion of *The Wrong Man*. Cary Grant is unmistakably the innocent party – a slightly supercilious advertising executive, suddenly plunged into a maelstrom of pursuit, a Kafkaesque comedy. The police of course will not believe Grant, even his mother will not believe him. In one delightful scene, which gleefully undermines the whole point of thriller movies (including

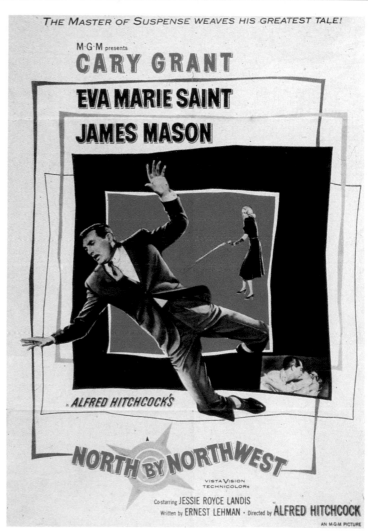

THE MASTER OF SUSPENSE WEAVES HIS GREATEST TALE!

M·G·M presents
CARY GRANT
EVA MARIE SAINT
JAMES MASON

ALFRED HITCHCOCK'S

NORTH BY NORTHWEST

VISTA VISION
TECHNICOLOR®
Co-starring JESSIE ROYCE LANDIS
Written by ERNEST LEHMAN · Directed by ALFRED HITCHCOCK
AN M-G-M PICTURE

Hitchcock's), Thornhill's mother turns to her son's pursuers in a crowded lift and laughingly inquires, 'You gentlemen aren't *really* trying to kill my son are you?' (One of Hitchcock's favorite venues for his macabre practical jokes was a crowded elevator. He was particularly fond of remarking to his companion on leaving as the doors closed 'I didn't think he would bleed so much!')

One of the best-remembered sequences from *North by Northwest* is Grant and Saint trapped on Mount Rushmore. Here Hitchcock, the expatriate English director, cheerfully flouts the American reverence for their national institutions. As in *Saboteur* with the Statue of Liberty Hitchcock extracts maximum mileage from his location at the climax of *North by Northwest*. The very idea of Cary Grant sheltering in the nostril of America's most venerated President while having a sneezing fit was too disrespectful to even contemplate. The nail-biting climax of the film is another masterly finale. Grant is frantically trying to grasp Saint's hand as she clings desperately onto the face of Mount Rushmore. It looks as though she will plunge to her death but Grant is determined to rescue her. In one swift cutaway, which manages to obviate the need for a great many convoluted explanations, we see Grant pulling her up onto the upper bunk of a railway sleeping car with the words 'Come on Mrs Thornhill.' Thus the audience knows that they escaped, are now safe, and have

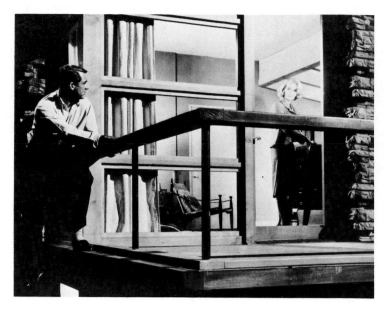

Above: *Cary Grant trying to rescue Eva Marie Saint from the clutches of enemy agents.*

married. The final scene, as the couple begin married life and the train plunges into a tunnel, is one of Hitchcock's most celebrated erotic images.

The overall effect of *North by Northwest* is a thrilling rollercoaster ride, supervised by a consummate professional. The film's reviews were fulsome. *Newsweek* said that *North by Northwest* 'resoundingly reaffirms the fact that Cary Grant and Alfred Hitchcock are two of the very slickest operators before and behind the Hollywood cameras. Together, they can be unbeatable.' The *New Yorker* astutely noticed that the film was 'a brilliant realization of a feat Hitchcock has been unintentionally moving toward for more than a decade – a perfect parody of his own work!' Ernest Lehman's script was nominated for an Oscar but the 1959 Awards were dominated by *Ben Hur*, which won a still unbeaten 11 Oscars.

Hitchcock returned to England to help promote the film, and while there agreed to be a castaway on British radio's longest running show, the perennial *Desert Island Discs*. The show's originator and host (until his death in 1984) Roy Plomley, recalled visiting Hitchcock's suite at Claridge's and being amazed at the director's flair for self-publicity. One of the standard questions was how the 'castaway' would cope with loneliness, to which Hitchcock replied, 'It's rather coincidental you should ask that because I've expressed my feelings in a picture I've just finished called *North by Northwest* . . .' Plomley remembered going along to see the film when it opened and being baffled as to what the film had to do with Alfred Hitchcock coping with loneliness on a desert island! Hitchcock's choice of records on *Desert Island Discs* was revealing – Gounod's *Funeral March of a Marionette* (which was the theme of his TV shows) was chosen because 'it does rather express my own attitude of treating the macabre with a sense of humor.' He also chose Wagner's *Siegfried's Horn Call* and pieces by Elgar, Schumann and Roussel. In fond memory of the music halls of his distant youth in London's East End, Hitchcock also chose George Robey's *The Fact Is* and Fred Emney's *A Sister to Assist 'er*. His chosen book, apart from the Bible and Shakespeare, was *Mrs Beeton's Household Management* and his one luxury was, enigmatically, a Continental Railway Timetable – shades of *The Lady Vanishes*?

Below: *The cliff-hanging climax to* North by Northwest.

Above: *The unmistakable Bates mansion from* Psycho *(1960).*
Below: *Anthony Perkins welcomes Janet Leigh to his cosy motel.*

Hitchcock's enjoyment in treating the macabre with a sense of humor was nowhere more apparent than in his last black-and-white film, *Psycho* (1960). The author of the original novel, Robert Bloch, was a prolific writer, concentrating on mystery and science-fiction stories, who had worked with Hitchcock on scripts for his television shows. However, to fashion the macabre story into a screenplay, Hitchcock commissioned a young, virtually untested writer, Joseph Stefano. Hitchcock delivered the screenplay to the offices of the Production Code and was surprised that their only objection was the use of the word 'transvestite' – ironic when you consider the savagery finally depicted onscreen! So it was that Hitchcock's most memorable murderer came into the world.

Norman Bates has entered the iconography of cinema. As recently as 1981 a British group called Landscape had a hit with a song called *Norman Bates*, the accompanying video was a loving homage to *Psycho*, with comedienne Pamela Stephenson in the Janet Leigh role. 'The Norman Bates High School' was an early tribute by director Brian de Palma in his film *Carrie* (1976). The Bates Motel was a pathetic, run-down place like the diner run by Lana Turner and Cecil Kellaway in *The Postman Always Rings Twice*, but the Psycho Mansion is still one of the main attractions on the tour around Universal Studios in Los Angeles.

Psycho is – ironically considering the critical pounding it received on release – the one film which the majority of people associate with Alfred Hitchcock, and that is largely due to one 45-second scene. Janet Leigh, tired after a long drive, decides to take a shower ... the shower scene from *Psycho* has become one of the best known in cinema's history, a scene remarkable for its ability to shock and disturb, even after repeated viewings. The actual shooting of this scene was

Above: *Probably the most famous film murder ever – the shower scene from* Psycho.
Right: *Norman Bates discovers the mysterious murder.*

undertaken by title designer Saul Bass under Hitchcock's direction, and Hitchcock would later explain with a lick of his lips that the 'blood' was actually chocolate sauce, because it looked better! The audience relaxes and unwinds with Leigh while she showers. She must be safe in the shower and she is, after all, the star of the film, so nothing can happen to *her*. Hitchcock may not have shared the reverence for stars but he recognized their uses. The star gives the audience a sense of security. If John Wayne, James Stewart or Clark Gable are there on screen, you know everything is going to be alright. This makes the impact of Leigh's death in *Psycho*, less than a third of the way into the film, all the more shocking. Even more shocking is the method of her death. Hitchcock himself was remarkably unflustered by the furore his scene caused; when told by a parent that his daughter refused to shower having seen *Psycho*, Hitch replied 'Have her dry cleaned!'

Leigh plays Marion Crane, who absconds with $40,000 of her employer's money, leaving behind her boyfriend Sam (John Gavin). On the run, she stays at Norman Bates' (Anthony Perkins) motel, where she is stabbed by an unknown 'woman' in the shower. Norman is terrified on discovering the body and puts it in Marion's car which he sinks in a nearby swamp. An investigator from the insurance company, Arbogast (Martin Balsam), tracks Marion's movements to the motel where his suspicions are aroused by

Norman. Shadowing him to the Bates Mansion, Arbogast is also murdered by the old woman. Meanwhile, also on the trail, Marion's sister Lila (Vera Miles) and Sam have learned that Norman's mother died in 1952. Investigating the old house, Lila is attacked in the cellar by 'Mrs Bates,' who of course turns out to be Norman in drag. The film ends with Norman twitching in a lunatic asylum, staring unblinking at the camera while his voice insists that he 'wouldn't even harm a fly.'

Bloch's novel was based on the true life story of a farmer, Ed Gein, who murdered 11 women in Wisconsin before his capture in 1957. The true story of Gein was too gruesome even for Hitchcock: Gein not only murdered the women, he cut up their bodies and covered furniture with their skin, he even wore the skin of his victims next to his own. Cinema audiences with a taste for 'authenticity' had to wait for Tobe Hooper's unsavory *Texas Chainsaw Massacre* (1974), which graphically depicted Gein's story.

By 1960 Janet Leigh was one of Hollywood's biggest female stars, so her untimely death in *Psycho* was a real shock, although she had a similar unpleasant experience in a motel two years before, in Orson Welles' masterly *film noir Touch of Evil* (1958). For Norman Bates Hitchcock chose Anthony Perkins, who became inseparable from the role and has never really escaped from Norman's shadow. He played the same role in *Psycho II* 22 years later, and is currently planning to star in and direct *Psycho III*.

Psycho was made for a paltry $800,000. Hitchcock had enjoyed the experience of working with a small crew and a low budget on his television shows, and he retained the same techniques, and largely the same crew, for *Psycho*. Shot in already unfashionable black and white, Hitchcock worked on the film quickly and in the strictest secrecy to maintain the shock effect of Leigh's premature murder. Hitchcock always maintained that the film was a 'fun picture' although the critics were brutal when dealing with the voyeurism of *Psycho*.

Hitchcock cast a blanket of secrecy around the film; critics were specifically asked in a letter from the director not to reveal the ending; and the public were not to be admitted after the film had begun. The trailer for the film, unlike the usually hyperbolic pieces boasting of the stars, spectacle and plot of next week's coming attraction, had Hitchcock taking the audience on a tour of the deserted Bates Mansion, dourly conducting his potential audience around the house like a ghoulish estate agent.

Reviews of the film were hostile (*Sight & Sound* airily dismissed it as 'a minor work') although nothing like as aggressive as those reserved for Michael Powell's *Peeping Tom* (1960) released later that year. In later years *Psycho* has been reappraised and proclaimed a classic. Reflecting on the critical reaction received by his films, Hitchcock wryly observed that his films 'went from being failures to masterpieces without ever being successes!' Commercially, however, *Psycho* was an immediate success and remains Hitchcock's most successful film. In 1960 it was second only to *Ben Hur* at the box office, taking nearly $9 million in its first year.

Hitchcock was in his sixties when *Psycho* was released. He had been making films for almost 40 years. He could well stand back and reflect upon his successful journey from Leytonstone to Hollywood. The few years preceding *Psycho* had been years of triumph, he had reached a pinnacle artistically and his financial future was secure. What that future held was uncertain.

Above: *Hitchcock passing an Italian window display of* Psycho, *his most successful film at the box office.*
Below: *A caricature of Hitchcock from around the time of* Psycho.

THE
GRAND OLD MAN

Below: *Hitchcock and one of the cast of* The Birds *(1963).*
Overleaf: *Poster from* The Birds *heralding Hitchcock's new protégé,*
Tippi Hedren.

"It could be
the most
terrifying
motion
picture
I have
ever made!"

Alfred Hitchcock

STARRING
ROD TAYLOR

JES

Screenplay by **EVAN HUNTER** · Direct

PLEASE DO NOT SEE THE E

ALFRED HITCHCOCK'S
"The Birds"

TECHNICOLOR

CERT
X
ADULTS ONLY

Based on Daphne Du Maurier's classic suspense story!

CA TANDY · SUZANNE PLESHETTE

and Introducing 'TIPPI' HEDREN

DISTRIBUTION

LFRED HITCHCOCK

O FIRST!!! See it from the beginning.

By the early 1960s cinema had changed. The Hollywood stranglehold had been broken by exciting and innovative work from Europe: directors like Truffaut, Louis Malle, Michelangelo Antonioni, Ingmar Bergman, Federico Fellini, Tony Richardson and Karel Reisz were establishing their reputations. The old-style Hollywood came to a tragic end with *The Misfits*, which proved to be the last film for both Clark Gable and Marilyn Monroe. Hitchcock, with veteran George Cukor, was one of the few directors still active who had made the transition from silent to sound cinema. He had since widely diversified his interests. While others feared the competition from television he had simply branched out to embrace it, establishing himself as master of another genre. When audiences paid to see an Alfred Hitchcock film, they knew what they were going to get, and for 40 years they had not been disappointed. But 1961 saw no film from the Master and neither did 1962 – they became the first years without a Hitchcock film since 1925. The three years between *Psycho* and Hitchcock's next film *The Birds* (1963) were frustrating ones for Hitchcock. No project interested him enough to start filming and *Psycho* was a pretty hard act to follow.

Looking for inspiration Hitchcock turned again to Daphne du Maurier, whose *Jamaica Inn* and *Rebecca* he had already filmed. She had originally published *The Birds* as a short story in 1952 and Hitchcock had purchased the film rights after reading it only once, immediately realizing the cinematic possibilities. It had lain dormant for a decade before his interest was reawakened by reports of birds attacking houses and animals on the West Coast. Typically, Hitchcock was not worried about the enormous technical difficulties posed by such a film. In one of his most celebrated *bon mots*, when asked by a journalist how he got the birds in the film to perform so well, Hitchcock deadpanned 'We paid them well.'

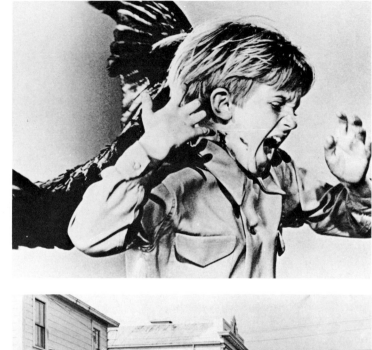

Top: *Publicity shot showing the threat of* The Birds.
Above center: *Hedren and Rod Taylor fleeing the birds' attack.*
Above: *Hedren in her first and most harrowing film role.*
Left: *Hitchcock in 1963.*

The short story deals with one farmer, Nat Hocken, and his family and is set in du Maurier's beloved rural Cornwall. The Hockens are besieged in their farmhouse, as millions of birds inexplicably start attacking humanity. The sheer weight of the birds destroys RAF planes, and the story ends bleakly with Nat smoking his last cigarette, the radio silent, and the birds outside massing for their final attack. Cinematically it presented a tantalizing problem, how to convey a world threatened by the most benign of creatures – birds. Of course, vultures in the desert, cadaverously eyeing the thirsty hero dragging himself across pitiless wastes are a screen cliché. Other threats by animal life have ranged from *King Kong* (1933) to the lamentable *The Swarm* (1978). But the idea of the end coming with millions of birds is not easy to accept, although one can see the appeal for Hitchcock, the filmmaker who specialized in seeing menace in the most unlikely places.

Hitchcock had his adaptator Evan Hunter (original author of the controversial *The Blackboard Jungle* and better known under his pseudonym, Ed McBain, as a writer of police thrillers) move the story from rural Cornwall to San Francisco and Bodega Bay, California. The birds attack a whole community in the film, rather than just one family. Of prime importance was the casting of the central character Melanie Daniels, and as in every film since 1951 (except for the quirky *The Trouble with Harry*) the girl had to be a blonde. Hitchcock was still looking for an actress he could cast in the Grace Kelly mold, and with Tippi Hedren he finally found one. Nathalie 'Tippi' Hedren was a model who Hitchcock and Alma spotted in a television drinks commercial in the early 1960s. At the age of 28 *The Birds* was to be her film debut. Hitchcock quite literally groomed her for stardom. He shot extensive screen tests, commissioned the illustrious Edith Head to design costumes specially for his new leading lady and built her up in a launch which recalled Selznick's build up of Scarlett O'Hara. It was typically perverse of Hitchcock that the vehicle he chose to launch his new discovery was one of the most physically arduous that any actress would ever undergo.

The crux of *The Birds* is that the animals in question are tame and docile, until they turn, with terrifying violence, against mankind. The transition has to be sharp and bloody. To emphasize that reversal, they have to be seen ferociously and unmistakably attacking Hedren and there can be no suggestion of trickery.

Melanie is fascinated by a young lawyer Mitch Brenner (Rod Taylor) whom she meets in San Francisco and joins on a visit to his young sister in Bodega Bay. On the way across the bay, Melanie is attacked by a swooping gull, the precursor of the war about to be waged by the birds. The gulls also attack a birthday party for Mitch's sister, and a neighboring farmer has his eyes gouged out by crows. Mitch and Melanie become trapped in the Brenner home, while the birds attack in squadrons, eventually breaking into an upstairs room and trapping Melanie. Rescued by Mitch, the family is driven away and the film's final, haunting image is of the birds brooding and waiting as the car drives off into the distance.

Like the stabbing scene in *Psycho*, which Janet Leigh recalled took a whole week to film, Tippi Hedren spent seven whole days trapped in a room on set doing nothing but being attacked by specially trained birds. Hitchcock would not even consider using a stand-in, or using mechanical birds, as originally intended. The whole week was literally torture for Tippi Hedren, and laid Hitchcock open to all sorts of accusa-

Above: *Production sketches for* The Birds.
Right: *Evan Hunter worked on the script of* The Birds.

Above: *Celebrating the launch of* The Birds *at the 1963 Cannes Film Festival.*

tions about his treatment of the new star, from the crew, contemporaries and future biographers. Tippi Hedren was so physically and mentally upset by her experiences that shooting of the film had to be suspended for a week. On-screen, of course, the finished result is tremendous, but one wonders how Hitchcock could justify such torment in the name of authenticity.

The gruelling scene of Melanie being attacked by the birds is perhaps one reason why this film disturbed Hitchcock more than any other in his career. He always saw filming as a job like any other, to be fitted into a nine-to-five working day and, despite the horror and suspense he so brilliantly evoked on the screen, Hitchcock was always able to switch off when he got home. Something in *The Birds* though cut through the cortex and Hitchcock confessed that he was 'tense and upset' during filming. It is du Maurier's vision and Hitchcock's

Below: *The petrol station inferno – the birds' first target.*

depiction of the way the world will end: not with the bang of a nuclear explosion, but with the whimper of birds flocking to attack.

The film's supreme technical achievements are not due to Hitchcock alone. He was helped enormously by Lawrence Hampton's special effects, Ray Berwick's bird training and Bernard Herrmann's eerie electronic score, quite startling in itself in the days before the electronic vagaries of Stockhausen were widely known.

The first sign of malign intent is the seemingly random attack on Melanie by a dipping gull, the sort of incident which can spoil a day in the middle of a holiday, but nothing more. As we begin to realize that this is only the beginning of something much more terrible, the thrust of Hitchcock's film is revealed. As the birds gain confidence and muster for ever larger and more ambitious attacks, he gradually builds up the suspense, always careful to prevent it boiling over into hysteria.

The gulls' attack on the petrol station is brilliantly filmed. A petrol pump attendant is knocked down by a gull and the petrol nozzle is left running, flooding the area with gasolene. A motorist entering his car pauses to light a cigar, customers in the cafe recognize the danger and scream a warning, but he is oblivious, lights his cigar, drops the match, and he and his car are enveloped in a massive explosion. Hitchcock also shows the scene from a bird's eye view – the town spread out below complete with blazing petrol station. The birds, having caused havoc, hover sinisterly above.

The most terrifying scene in the film has Mrs Brenner discovering the dead farmer, whose eyes have been gouged out. We sense something is wrong, the birds have already displayed their potential menace, and as she slowly makes her way through the apparently normal house, the suspense builds unbearably; having discovered the body she drives off in her truck at great speed. Even a straightforward scene like the arrival and departure of the truck from the farm is brilliantly handled by Hitchcock – for Mrs Brenner's arrival

Hitchcock had the dusty road watered down, but for the departure, the dust flew up, emphasizing the panic and speed of her escape. There is another nicely handled moment when Melanie is trapped by the birds in a telephone booth, recalling the earlier description of her as 'a bird in a gilded cage.'

Hitchcock's best films shock and stun with their overall impact but it is only after repeated viewing (Hitchcock himself felt that his films had to be seen at least three times to be fully appreciated) that one notices these nice little touches which make just as much of a contribution to the richness of the finished film. Sadly, even Hitchcock could not bring off his idea for the final image of the film. He wanted to show Melanie and Mitch escaping to San Francisco – only to find the Golden Gate Bridge completely covered in birds.

Hitchcock went straight from the impending Armageddon of *The Birds* to *Marnie* (1964) which was based on a novel by Winston Graham (best known for his *Poldark* novels which became a successful TV series in the late 1970s). Hitchcock's main interest in the film lay in the fact that finally he had managed to lure Grace Kelly back to the screen after an absence of six years.

Hollywood was delighted when in 1956, in what was called the marriage of the decade, Grace Kelly married Prince Rainier. The Hitchcocks were one of the few couples from Grace's 'former life' that her husband would entertain in Monaco, and Hitchcock had never given up trying to coerce

Top: *Poster for* Marnie *(1964)*
Above: *Tippi Hedren as Marnie, her second film for Hitchcock.*

Above: *Fresh from James Bond, Sean Connery (center) in* Marnie.
Left: *Hedren as the kleptomaniac Sean Connery is determined to save.*
Below: *Marnie in strictly equine mood.*

the Princess back to the screen. In March 1962 a statement was issued from the Royal Palace in Monaco announcing that: 'Her Serene Highness would play the lead in Alfred Hitchcock's new film *Marnie* . . . Her Highness will return to Monaco with her family in November.' No one had anticipated the outcry which followed. Monaco's inhabitants were stunned, they felt that Grace's standing as a Catholic Princess would be severely undermined by returning to the vulgarity of the cinema screen. Despite Princess Grace's announcement that her fee would be donated to children's charities in Monaco, the furore did not abate. Eventually, Princess Grace issued a statement saying that she would decline the role because she had been 'very influenced by the reaction which the announcement provoked in Monaco.' Hitchcock was deeply upset, and Princess Grace, who died tragically in 1982, never seriously considered returning to the screen again.

Hitchcock found solace in the fact that the eponymous heroine of his new film would now be played by his latest protégée, Tippi Hedren. Ever-conscious of the box office, he was delighted to be working with Sean Connery, who was in the ascendant after starring as James Bond in *Doctor No* (1962) and *From Russia with Love* (1963). Hitchcock appreciated Connery's professionalism, while Connery was eager to escape, albeit briefly, the mantle of 007. Director John Boorman recalled an anecdote Sean Connery told him about Hitchcock: 'Hitch had developed a kind of code for talking to actors, which he hated doing. At one point he interrupted Sean with the simple phrase "Dog's feet!" and then walked away. Connery thought about this . . . "Dog's feet?" . . . "paws" . . . "ah yes . . . Pause!"'

Above: *Sean Connery trying to relax a tense Tippi Hedren.*
Below: *Hitchcock instructing his two principals on set.*

Above: *Marnie with her beloved horse and her not-so-beloved husband.*
Right: *Marnie caught red-handed.*

'Marnie' Edgar is a young, beautiful kleptomaniac. She steals from businessman Mark Rutland (Connery) and disappears. But Mark is fascinated by her and tracks her down, then, hoping to put her back on the straight and narrow, he forces her to marry him. Marnie, however, is frigid and attempts suicide. Determined to understand his wife, Mark tracks down her mother, who was a prostitute, and discovers that as a child Marnie killed an aggressive client, an incident she has effectively blocked out of her memory. Mark reveals all this to his wife, hoping to lead her away from kleptomania and toward a new life.

It is a stagy, flimsily psychological thriller, with Hitchcock seeming to derive some perverse pleasure from making it appear as artificial as possible – the back projection is obvious and the painted backdrops look totally false. Hitchcock was attracted to the film by the idea of Mark's fetish for sleeping with a thief! In *Marnie* he catches his thief, but Marnie's frigidity threatens to destroy their relationship. The underlying sexuality of the whole film is manifest.

Marnie divided Hitchcock's followers, many felt that it was a vulgar exercise. But in recent years the film – like so many of his works – has been reappraised, although the apologia seems perverse. Philip Strick wrote: 'If one symbol had to be selected to summarize the Hitchcock message in half a century of film-making, it should not, in fact, be one of mayhem, as the maestro would undoubtedly have recommended. More

accurately it would be the sight of Marnie being led by the hand toward the possibility of a new life!' Hitchcock's use of color in the film was exemplary and Marnie's aversion to the color red (a result of her childhood killing) is well handled. Also delicately handled is the reunion between Marnie and her mother (Louise Latham). When Marnie asks pitifully, 'You must have loved me, Mamma?' she replies touchingly, 'Why, sugar-plum, you're the only thing I ever did love. I just

Above: *A reflective Hitchcock from the early 1960s.*

never knew how to tell you.' The child's *need* for the love of the parent is one of the great truths of life and a theme with which films have dealt from *East of Eden* (1955) to the Oscar-laden *Terms of Endearment* (1983), but it is an unusual subject for Alfred Hitchcock. At best *Marnie* is a very interesting failure, but it is a very minor Hitchcock.

The downward spiral continued with *Torn Curtain* (1966), an orthodox Iron Curtain thriller which Hitchcock tackled uncomfortably. Politics had never played a large part in his films – the MacGuffin usually kept political aspects at a suitably hazy distance. Hitchcock was familiar with the story of the defecting British spies Burgess and Maclean; forsaking their country, betraying their class, they fled to Russia in 1951, to be followed in 1963 by 'The Third Man,' Kim Philby. The Burgess and Maclean case had a massive effect on Britain in the 1950s. The Cold War hostility was already apparent, but it was still hard to believe that the two traitors could so willingly have betrayed their country and settled in Russia. Hitchcock said that what appealed to him initially about the project was 'what did Mrs Maclean think of the whole thing?' In fact, she soon deserted her husband in Russia and went on to marry Philby. The dramatic possibilities of the story were brilliantly explored in Alan Bennett's *An Englishman Abroad*, made for television in 1983 and dealing with Burgess' exile in Moscow. While in 1977 *Philby, Burgess and Maclean* (also made for TV) saw Derek Jacobi and Anthony Bate give mesmerizing performances.

Hitchcock's fascination with defecting spies continued to the end of his life, and his very last screen treatment – never filmed – was about the spy George Blake, who escaped from

Top: *Poster heralding Hitchcock's 50th film.*
Left: *The realistically difficult murder scene from* Torn Curtain *(1966).*
Opposite, both: *The star of* Torn Curtain *was Paul Newman, an actor with whom Hitchcock had little in common.*

prison in Britain in 1966 and fled to Russia. So a film about Burgess and Maclean and the extent of their betrayal of the British upper classes should have been an ideal project, added to which spies and spying retain a huge fascination for the public. Indeed, when Hitchcock was filming *Torn Curtain* the screen had already seen spies like Len Deighton's Harry Palmer, John Le Carré's Alec Leamass and Ian Fleming's James Bond establish themselves. Sadly, none of this was realized in *Torn Curtain*. In an appreciation of Paramount Pictures, the film is dismissed as 'a flaccidly directed thriller, overburdened with too many clichés and the miscasting and mismatching of its stars!'

Michael Armstrong (Paul Newman) is an American atomic scientist who pretends to defect in order to obtain a valuable top-secret formula from a professor in East Germany. The plot is complicated when Armstrong's fiancée Sarah Sherman (Julie Andrews) believes his 'defection,' and follows him across the Iron Curtain. Armstrong is forced to kill a bodyguard before he and Sarah can escape their pursuers at a ballet performance and finally return to the West on a Scandinavian ship.

The film boded well when Hitchcock got as his two stars Paul Newman and Julie Andrews. Andrews had just come from *The Sound of Music* (1965), already on its way to becoming the most successful film since *Gone with the Wind*;

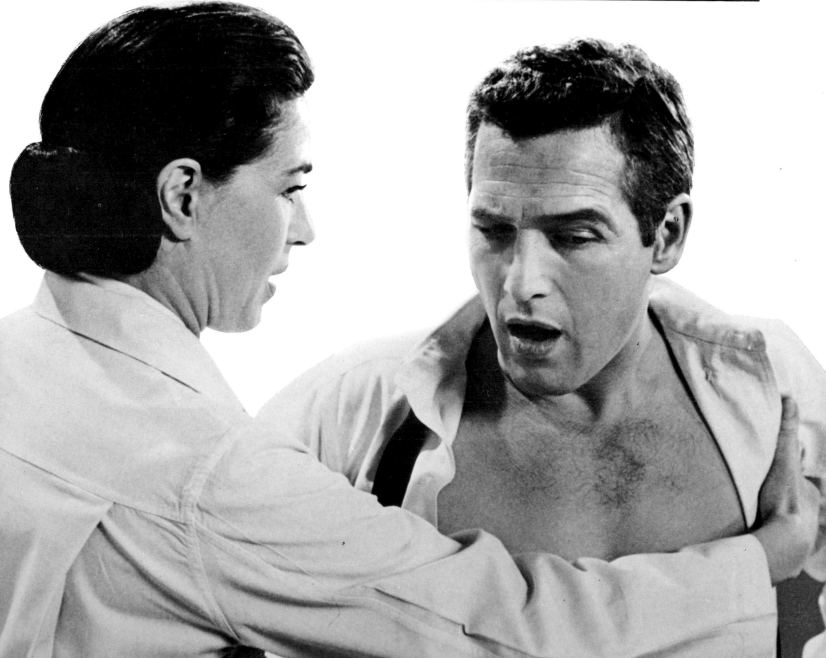

and Newman had proved himself one of Hollywood's most articulate and intense stars, as well as one of the most durable. His work is characterized by a determination and uncompromising integrity, with films like *The Hustler* (1961) and *Cool Hand Luke* (1967) to his credit. Newman has proved himself over 30 years of film superstardom, but there was not a happy atmosphere between him and Hitchcock. Newman had begun his career as an actor steeped in the Method, and his rise to stardom started when he took over roles originally destined for James Dean before his untimely death in 1955. Hitchcock also found Newman's casual approach to life hard to swallow: one night at dinner with the Hitchcocks, Newman unforgivably declined the vintage wine and insisted on drinking beer from a can! The film was not a happy experience for any of the principals. Hitchcock told the cast on the first day that he found the process of filming boring, which Julie Andrews found disheartening. With Newman the clashes were artistic. Hitchcock found his methods of preparing for a scene time-consuming and unnecessary and in the end Newman's performance was oddly stilted and mannered.

Torn Curtain was Hitchcock's 50th film, as the publicists never tired of pointing out. But by this time the director was facing considerable opposition – from himself! The name

Below: *Julie Andrews and Paul Newman behind the Iron Curtain.*

Alfred Hitchcock had become synonymous with cinema thrillers and directors had always tried to mimic his style. There were now many valiant stabs at filming in the tradition of Hitchcock – Roman Polanski's *Repulsion* (1965), William Wyler's *The Collector* (1965), Jules Dassin's *Topkapi* (1964), Stanley Donen's *Charade* (1964) and Mark Robson's *The Prize* (1963) had all appeared by the time of *Torn Curtain*, and all bore Hitchcock hallmarks. But now for the first time the real thing in the shape of *Torn Curtain* came as a disappointment. The increasingly stylish James Bond thrillers, which owed a great debt to Hitchcock before they went on to become nonsensical exercises in gadgetry, showed how tightly paced thrillers, written with wit and style, could hold an audience's attention. Polanski's *Repulsion* dwelt on the borders of *Psycho* territory, and even *The Prize* (also starring Paul Newman) was a far better example of a Hitchcock picture than the current real thing.

Even on its release *Torn Curtain* looked dated and stilted. All the 'East European' locations were shot on the Universal lot and while the critics were on the whole respectful, their real enthusiasm was now reserved for Hitchcock's disciples. Everyone was agreed though that one scene – when Paul Newman murders the bodyguard – showed the Master's old touch. Before gratuitous and graphic violence filled the cinema screens in the late 1960s and early 1970s, onscreen murder was usually a pretty restrained business; even Hitchcock felt that the shower murder in *Psycho* would have

been too much if it had been filmed in color. Talking about the slow, detailed killing in *Torn Curtain*, Hitchcock told Truffaut: 'I thought it was time to show that it was very difficult, very painful and it takes a very long time to kill a man ... the killing has to be carried out by means suggested by the locale and the characters ... so we use household objects: the kettle full of soup, a carving knife, a shovel, and, finally, a gas oven.' It is a terrifying scene, brilliantly filmed and edited; conveying the very difficulty that many of Hitchcock's central figures – 'ordinary' people, unused to the sordid business of murder – would experience. Despite its shortcomings, the film was a success on its release; the box-office potential of Andrews and Newman had not been overrated, and Hitchcock's name could still pull in the crowds. Together they ensured that *Torn Curtain* was the seventh most successful film in America that year.

Hitchcock felt threatened by films which appeared bearing all his hallmarks, a situation not helped by the hostile reviews which greeted *Torn Curtain*. Hitchcock was 70 when he began work on his 51st film in the late 1960s; and his critical reputation had been diving steadily since *Psycho* nearly a decade before. He was an old man in a world which had changed enormously in a very short space of time. That decade will always be remembered as 'The Swinging Sixties,'

Below: *Hitchcock's cameo from* Topaz *(1969).*   Above: *A still from Hitchcock's lackluster* Topaz.

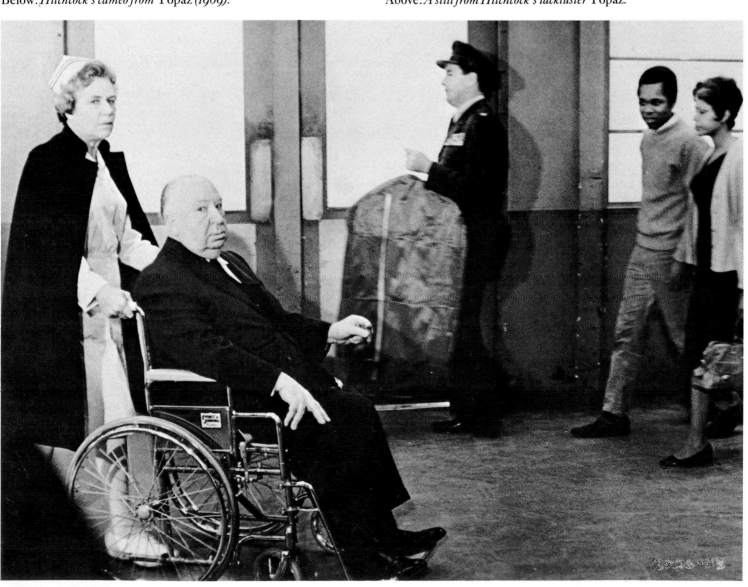

Top: *A revolutionary scene from* Topaz.
Above: *Karin Dor and Frederic Stafford in a love scene.*
Above right: *The murder scene for which* Topaz *is best remembered.*

and to really 'live' during the 1960s you just *had* to be young. 1969 was the year of Woodstock and *Easy Rider*; Hitchcock's *Topaz* sat uneasily amid films like *Midnight Cowboy* and *Alice's Restaurant*.

Hitchcock had been desperately casting around for a suitable subject to film and eventually settled, grudgingly, on Leon Uris' best seller based upon the events of the Cuban Missile Crisis seven years before. Uris' novels had been

filmed before – *The Angry Hills* (1959) and, notably, *Exodus* (1960) by Otto Preminger. Uris' books were guaranteed blockbusters, well-researched novels set against sprawling historical canvases, ideal airport reading but totally unsuitable for a film by Alfred Hitchcock.

The plot of *Topaz* (1969) is a complex one, involving a Communist organization at the heart of NATO, and an anti-Castro faction at work in Cuba at the height of the 1962 Missile Crisis, which brought the world to the brink of nuclear war. Here the day of judgment will come with a 'bang'; the whimper of *The Birds* is long ago and far away. While Kennedy and Khrushchev played at political brinkmanship, for 13 perilous days the fate of the world hung in the balance. It is an exciting background for a spy film, and one can imagine the relish with which a storyteller like Frederick Forsyth would have tackled the project. But Hitchcock's finished film is dated in a most unnostalgic way and none of the characters comes alive. The cast is largely undistinguished, although John Forsythe makes a welcome reappearance following his earnest portrayal of the young artist in *The Trouble with Harry*, and Dany Robin, who had appeared with some distinction in *The Waltz of the Toreadors* (1962), was an attractive leading lady.

During filming, Hitchcock said that *Topaz* reminded him of *Notorious*: 'It's a story about espionage in high places, and deals with the top echelon of intelligence agents. It shows how the real dirty work is done by the lower echelon people with the top people pressing the buttons as it were.' Such themes have been tackled effectively on film, notably in the Harry Palmer films, *The Ipcress File* (1965) and *Funeral in Berlin* (1967) (both based on the Len Deighton books and steeped in conflict between Michael Caine's resentful decidedly working-class agent and his urbane, upper-class controllers), and Sidney Lumet's *The Deadly Affair* (1966). But Hitchcock's *Topaz* is an antediluvian piece about espionage, with the Communists no more convincing than boogeymen! On his death the Soviet newspaper *Literaturnaya Gazeta* castigated Hitchcock as a director whose work glorified viciousness and cruelty, reflecting the moral, social and

Above: *Hitchcock on the set of* Topaz *with Karin Dor.*

Below: *John Vernon (third from left) and Karin Dor in* Topaz.

UNIVERSAL PRESENTS
ALFRED HITCHCOCK'S
"TOPAZ" A
From the Novel by Leon Uris   TECHNICOLOR ®
Starring FREDERICK STAFFORD · DANY ROBIN · JOHN VERNON
KARIN DOR · MICHEL PICCOLI
PHILIPPE NOIRET and JOHN FORSYTHE
Screenplay by SAMUEL TAYLOR
Directed by ALFRED HITCHCOCK

psychological decay of Western society, and singled out the 'anti-Soviet' *Torn Curtain* and *Topaz* for 'erasing the distinction between moral and immoral, and parading the pathological and sadism as an everyday norm.'

Hitchcock recalled that *Topaz* was 'a most unhappy picture to make.' The unhappiness and dissatisfaction are reflected by the finished film; the two hours and four minutes it runs seem like purgatory. Only once does Hitchcock perform a sleight of hand which recalls the autograph of the Master in happier days. Juanita (Karin Dor) is murdered by one of Castro's henchmen; she wears a beautiful, trailing purple gown and while her executioner talks to her the camera travels until it is directly overhead. She is suddenly shot, falling to the floor, while her gown spreads out around her like a blossoming flower. But one shot does not a great film make, and *Topaz* is best swiftly passed over.

Hitchcock's career was in the doldrums, he had not made a film worthy of his name in nearly 10 years. There were many who felt that after *Topaz* he was past it and that honorable retirement was the best option. Hitchcock was taking longer between films, there just did not seem to be the right properties for development. Hitchcock rarely read any fiction, because he was always imagining how the novel would look on screen, but as the world's most famous film director he was, of course, inundated with scripts, novels and ideas. But Hitchcock was more than ever constrained by his own reputation and so few people bothered to think what his films were actually like before submitting their material. Hitchcock complained to Truffaut: 'You are a free person to make whatever you want. I, on the other hand, can only make what

Above: *Karin Dor and John Vernon and* (opposite) *Frederick Stafford and Dany Robin from* Topaz, *Hitchcock's last film of the 1960s.*

is expected of me, that is, a thriller or suspense story, and that I find hard to do. So many stories seem to be about neo-Nazis, Palestinians fighting Israelis and all that kind of thing. And, you see, none of those subjects have any human conflict.'

Hitchcock was always keen to delineate the difference between mystery and suspense. He felt that suspense necessitated that 'the public be made perfectly aware of all the facts involved . . . mystery is seldom suspenseful. In a whodunnit, for instance, there is no suspense, but a sort of intellectual puzzle. The whodunnit generates the kind of curiosity that is void of emotion, and emotion is an essential ingredient of suspense.' To actor Michael Wilding he confided that the secret of creating suspense in a film was 'never to begin a scene at the beginning and never to let it go on to the end!' Authors and scriptwriters commonly made the mistake of thinking Hitchcock was a whodunnit type of filmmaker, whereas in the majority of his films the identity of the murderer is apparent from the very beginning. His main theme is of the innocent on the run (*The 39 Steps, Saboteur, North by Northwest*) or 'just how far can you take a character before he is unmasked?' (exemplified by *Sabotage, Suspicion* and *Shadow of a Doubt*). Hitchcock's main enjoyment as a director was still the fugues he could play in his films, how he could manipulate his audiences, how far he could take them.

Hitchcock in the late 1960s being made an Officer of the French Order of Arts and Letters, presented by Francois Truffaut.

COMING HOME

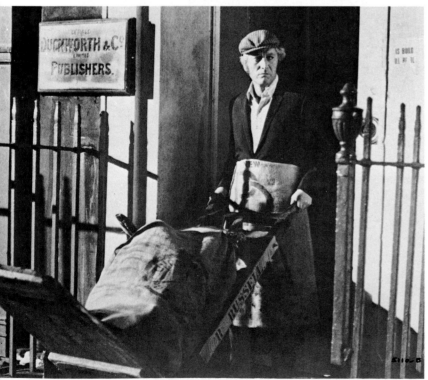

Top: *Hitchcock on location in Covent Garden, filming in London for the first time in over 20 years.*
Above: *Barry Foster disposing of the evidence in* Frenzy *(1972).*

When Alfred Hitchcock returned to his native London to make his first film there in over 20 years, it was a triumphant homecoming. Hitchcock's attention had finally settled on a modest little thriller by Arthur LaBern *Goodbye Piccadilly, Farewell Leicester Square*, which he asked playwright Anthony Shaffer to adapt for the screen. Shaffer (brother of Peter, author of *Amadeus*) was exactly the right choice for scriptwriter; his play *Sleuth* was a demonically clever thriller and was released as a film in 1972 – the same year as *Frenzy* which was to become Hitchcock's 52nd film. The combination of Hitchcock and Shaffer proved irresistible. Despite Hitchcock's disappointing track record over the preceding 10 years, the press welcomed him 'home' with great affection.

Hitchcock arrived in London in mid-1971, installed himself and Alma in his favorite suite at Claridges, and set about casting for his new film, drawing from a strong new breed of English performers coming into their own on the London stage. The two main characters were played by Barry Foster and Jon Finch. Foster had been successfully psychopathic in *Twisted Nerve* (1968) and later went on to great fame as the detective in the TV series *Van Der Valk*. Finch was an edgily ambitious Macbeth in Roman Polanski's 1971 film. When asked why he was not using 'star' names for *Frenzy*, Hitchcock calculatingly replied: 'You take an unknown actor. If he doesn't work out, you get rid of him!' For the supporting cast, Hitchcock assembled a stellar collection of British talent – Billie Whitelaw, Anna Massey, Clive Swift, Alec McCowen and Vivien Merchant.

Filming *Frenzy* gave Hitchcock the opportunity to revisit the London of his youth. Much of the location work took place in Covent Garden, the capital's traditional fruit and vegetable market, scene of *My Fair Lady* and where Hitchcock's greengrocer father made regular journeys at the turn of the century. The market had not changed much, but was under threat of demolition. Like Smithfield meat market, Covent Garden was a world of its own; because of the early start even the pubs opened at 5am. Whole families had worked and lived there for generations and Hitchcock made the most of the location filming, revelling in the opportunity to film – perhaps for the last time – a unique world at the very heart of London. At the opening of *Frenzy* Hitchcock reflected another traditional aspect of London, filming outside County Hall. It was also the building glimpsed from Scotland Yard at the very end of *Blackmail* 43 years before.

Richard Blaney (Jon Finch) is a dissolute former Squadron Leader who is suspected of being London's necktie murderer when his former wife Brenda (Barbara Leigh-Hunt) is found strangled with a tie similar to one of Blaney's around her neck. Then Blaney's mistress Babs (Anna Massey) is found murdered in a similar fashion and he goes into hiding with his old friend Bob Rusk (Barry Foster). Eventually caught by the police, and after a trial at the Old Bailey, Blaney is sentenced to life imprisonment. But Inspector Oxford (Alec McCowen) has his doubts about Blaney's guilt; even after Blaney escapes from prison, Oxford is convinced of his innocence. Eventually Blaney makes his way to Rusk's flat, where Oxford is waiting, and Rusk is revealed to be the murderer.

The film was budgeted at a modest $2 million (and went on to make a respectable $15 million). Hitchcock was particularly proud of his use of natural sound on the London locations and his ability to avoid the use of cliché. Like the 'blossoming flower' murder of *Topaz*, *Frenzy* is best remembered for an audacious long, slow track away from the scene of Babs' murder. Rusk takes her to his flat to murder her, ushering her in with a sinister 'You know, you're my kind of woman.' The camera leaves it there, and begins its slow, stately pull back down the stairs and into the street, until it is on the opposite pavement. All the while, the soundtrack is filled with the growing roar of traffic, leaving the murder entirely to the imagination.

It is exactly this type of restraint which, prior to *Frenzy*, had been one of Hitchcock's strongest weapons – one recalls the torture scene in *Foreign Correspondent*, when it is what is not shown that makes the scene so effective. Hitchcock's supreme achievement was to use the imaginations of his audience to do his work for him – he just set the scene. This touch of genius contrasts oddly with the graphic depictions of other murders which jar throughout *Frenzy*. The year of *Frenzy* was also the year of *Straw Dogs* and *The Devils*, the two most extreme examples of the new 'pornography of violence'; Hitchcock seemed to be trying to prove that at 73 he could still be as contemporary as the new blood-and-guts breed. So *Frenzy* comes complete with gratuitous sex and violence. Rusk's murder of Barbara is grisly; she recites the 91st Psalm as she is raped to his gloating cries of 'lovely . . . lovely,' and in an effort to retrieve the tell-all tiepin which will reveal him as the murderer, Rusk has to crack open the fingers of a corpse in which rigor mortis has already set in.

Right: *Hitchcock at a press conference in London for the opening of* Frenzy. *It proved a commercial success.*
Below: *Close up of the unusually explicit murder in his penultimate film.*

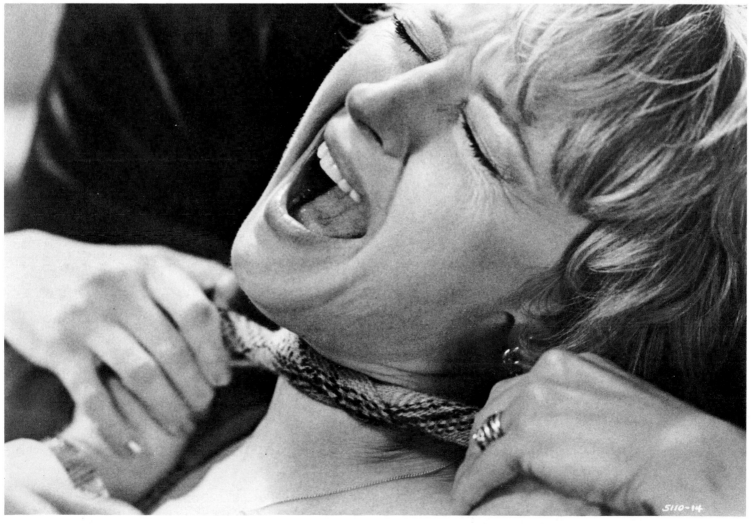

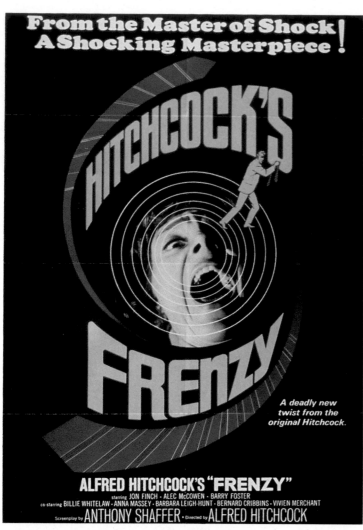

Opposite: *Barry Foster revealed as 'The Necktie Murderer.'*
Left: *Poster for* Frenzy *(1972).*
Above: *William Devane examines his ill-gotten gains in* Family Plot
(1976), Hitchcock's last film.
Below: *Devane's accomplice, Karen Black.*

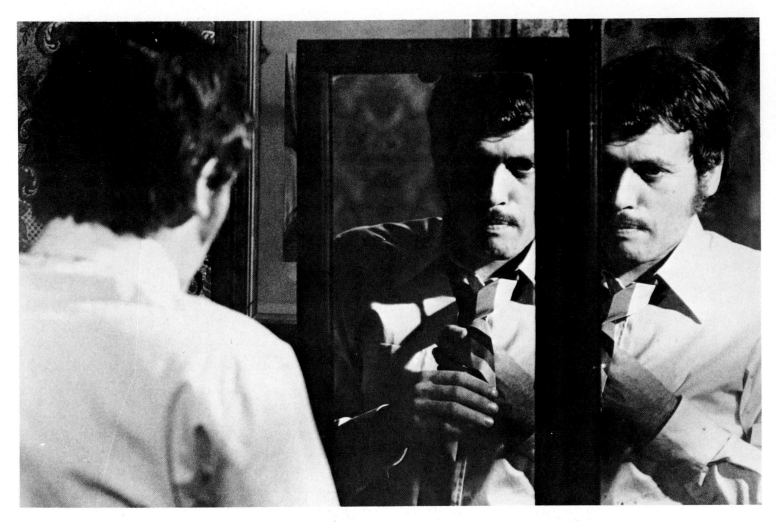

Above: *Jon Finch as the chief suspect in* Frenzy.
Bottom right: *Hitchcock accepting his honorary Oscar, 1967.*

The 1971 London of *Frenzy* is really the London of Hitchcock's memory. Despite set pieces at the Hilton Hotel, decimal coinage and the gratuitous frankness about sex, *Frenzy* is rooted in the same era as *Stage Fright* and *The Paradine Case*. Jon Finch is simply far too young to play a retired Squadron Leader, and the whole film has a feel of the late 1940s about it, as if Hitchcock expected Johnny and Beaky from *Suspicion* to drop in at any moment! By 1971, the impact of World War II on London was largely lost, the effects of the terrible bombing had been largely eradicated by rising tower blocks, but Hitchcock set the bulk of his film in Covent Garden – a part of London that had not changed since George Bernard Shaw's *Pygmalion*. In his review of the film Alexander Walker wrote: 'It looks – even more, it sounds – as if Mr Chamberlain is still Prime Minister and Mrs Miniver rules over the country (but) the grisliness of the murders is straight out of the permissive 1970s.' That air of cosy nostalgia permeates the film's policemen – Oxford and his sergeant are straight out of Tom Stoppard's *The Real Inspector Hound*. Even here Hitchcock exercises his inventiveness in one way, which avoids long and dull expository sequences of Oxford explaining his doubts to his superiors at New Scotland Yard. He has to endure his wife's (Vivien Merchant's) gourmet efforts, when all he longs for is shepherd's pie or bacon and eggs. As his wife lovingly serves up grisly looking attempts at cordon bleu, Oxford moves the plot forward by confiding in her through gritted teeth. Amid the incongruity of graphic rape and murders set uneasily in the atmosphere of affability and nostalgia which permeates *Frenzy*, these little scenes are wryly handled and come as welcome light relief.

While *Frenzy* is by no means vintage Hitchcock, it merits a place in his canon for its loving depiction of a London long gone and for proving he was still capable of making diverting, thoroughly entertaining films into his seventies. 'A connoisseur's piece, with echoes right back to *The Lodger* . . .' *Sight & Sound* called the picture, and indeed critically and commercially *Frenzy* put Hitchcock back in the running. His reputation was once again in the ascendant and he was showered with praise and critical re-evaluations, the like of which he had not seen since the heady days of the 1950s.

While his 'disciples' continued to make films in the Hitchcock tradition but concentrating more on the psychological elements of the stories than on the characters or suspense angles, Hitchcock maintained quite rightly: 'An audience must have information if they are to care about the characters. There are too many so-called "mystery" films today: half the time you don't know who the people are or what they're doing. Nowadays there are too few films and too many photographs of people talking!' While such sentiments may sound like the ill-informed opinions of an aging filmmaker, yearning for the simplicity and straightforwardness of 'the good old days,' Hitchcock was in fact an astute director and observer. Too many directors in the mid-1970s mistook the new liberalism as an excuse for an all or nothing style of filmmaking. For every disturbing masterpiece like Stanley Kubrick's *A Clockwork Orange* (1971) there were half a hundred cash-ins. Thrillers relied on star names, convoluted plots and inaudible dialogue.

Hitchcock was determined to keep on working. Alma, though having suffered a stroke during *Frenzy*, was recovering and urging Hitch to read new novels, determined to keep his interest alive. Hitchcock could of course afford to retire. He was still getting repeat fees for *Alfred Hitchcock Presents* and between 1960 and 1962 launched *The Alfred Hitchcock Hour* on television, although he only actually directed one show. His name had become synonymous with horror and suspense and a steady flow of endorsements came his way, including *The Alfred Hitchcock Mystery Magazine* and a series of horror short story books, with titles like *Tales My Mother Never Told Me*. As producer of his own films, Hitchcock of course received income from their theatrical releases and television screenings. An astute business move some years before had seen Hitchcock become a large shareholder in the massive entertainments corporation, MCA. But when asked if he planned to retire, his standard response was still 'What for? What to?'

Incredibly, Hitchcock had never won an Oscar for Best Director and only *Rebecca*, of all his films over the years, won a Best Picture award, which was received by Selznick, the producer. In 1967, though, Hitchcock was honored by the Academy when he was presented with the Irving Thalberg Memorial Award. While the Oscars may have eluded him other bodies have showered him with honors. In 1972 Hitchcock became the first film personality to receive an Honorary Degree from Columbia University; he was also awarded an Honorary Doctorate from the University of Southern California. The culmination came in 1974 when Hitchcock was honored by the Film Society at the Lincoln Center in New York. The occasion was celebrated by a glittering array of celebrities including Grace Kelly, Joan Fontaine and Janet Leigh, who turned out to pay tribute to Hitchcock as one of cinema's immortals. Quite unlike any of the artists previously honored in this way Hitchcock, at the grand old age of 75, was still working.

Above: *Hitchcock receiving another honor from his French acolytes, presented by actress Jeanne Moreau in 1969.*
Below: *Hitchcock in London while filming* Frenzy.

Above: *Hitchcock, flanked by Grace Kelly and Alma, at the 1972 Cannes Film Festival.*
Below: *Hitchcock kissing Edith Head, costume designer on many of his films. She won many awards for her designs.*
Left: *With gigantic birthday cake.*
Opposite: *Receiving his Honorary Doctorate from Columbia University, in New York, 1972.*

*The Film Society of
Lincoln Center* in cooperation with

The Museum of Modern Art,

Lincoln Center for the Performing Arts and

City Center of Music and Drama

welcomes Alfred Hitchcock

at this evening's gala in his honor

Monday, April 29, 1974 at 9pm

at Avery Fisher Hall, Lincoln Center

Right: *Poster for a Gala honoring
Hitchcock in his 75th year.*
Above: *Hitchcock shaking hands with
birthday guest Charlton Heston.*

Above: *Hitchcock's apposite final cameo in* Family Plot *(1976).*

Hitchcock was back in top gear. Chancing upon a novel by Victor Canning, *The Rainbird Pattern*, Hitchcock was immediately fascinated by the cinematic possibilities of two parallel narratives converging. He contacted Ernest Lehman, and convinced him that the book offered them an opportunity to pull off again what they had achieved with *North by Northwest*. In March 1975 filming began on Alfred Hitchcock's 53rd film, now entitled *Family Plot* (1976).

The film is a difficult one to condense, as it follows two totally different strands of narrative, only joining them together some way into the film. Spiritualist Blanche Tyler (Barbara Harris) and her boyfriend George Lumley (Bruce Dern) are asked by rich spinster Julia Rainbird (Cathleen Nesbitt) to try and find her heir, a nephew who has been missing since childhood. Simultaneously, Arthur Adamson (William Devane) and Fran (Karen Black) are undertaking a series of bizarre kidnaps and jewel thefts. Eventually, the paths of the two couples irrevocably entwine and it is revealed that Adamson is the missing heir. However, afraid that they will discover his criminal activities, Adamson tries to murder Blanche and George. Eventually they escape, trapping Adamson and Fran who are then arrested. For their efforts, Blanche and George are well rewarded by Miss Rainbird.

For *Family Plot* Hitchcock again chose relatively new faces rather than established star names. Bruce Dern had worked with the director once before, his second film appearance had been a tiny role in *Marnie* (1964). By 1976 he was on the way to becoming one of American cinema's more interesting actors, he had enjoyed working with Jack Nicholson on *Drive, He Said* (1970) and *The King of Marvin Gardens* (1972) and had won high praise for his stubborn performance in *The Great Gatsby* (1974). Barbara Harris had made the quirky *A Thousand Clowns* (1965) and Robert Altman's sprawling epic *Nashville* (1975) but few other films. William Devane was brought in to replace Roy Thinnes a month after shooting began; his background was again largely stage and television but he went on to star, to great effect, in *Yanks* (1979) alongside Vanessa Redgrave. Karen Black had appeared with distinction in *The Day of the Locust* (1975) after establishing a sensuous reputation in the film of the controversial *Portnoy's Complaint* (1972). For the role of Julia Rainbird, Hitchcock selected the eminent actress Cathleen Nesbitt, a beauty of the Edwardian stage, who had been the one great love of the poet Rupert Brooke, and was into her eighties when she began filming. Bruce Dern frankly admitted that out of the 30 films he had made to date, Hitchcock was without doubt the best director he had ever worked with. The largely young cast, in awe of the old master and his reputation for restricting actors, found working with him produced quite the opposite effect, and thoroughly enjoyed the experience.

Above: *A portrait of Hitchcock in 1969. Then aged 70, he was still working.*

Hitchcock was a spritely but unbowed 76 when filming *Family Plot* on location in San Francisco and on the Universal lot. Steven Spielberg, the most successful film director of all time and a 'major fan' of Hitchcock's work, had tried to see him at work on *Torn Curtain* in 1966, when as a precocious 19-year-old he had connived his way on set, only to be promptly evicted. Spielberg recalled thinking: '*Jaws* is on release, and Hitchcock is shooting *Family Plot*. I thought "Great, finally I get my chance to watch Hitchcock." So I walk on set and he's sitting with his back 100% to me. There's no possible way he could see me. All of a sudden he waves an arm in the air to an assistant director, who walks over. Hitchcock talks to him, then gets up and leaves the sound stage *very* quickly. He could walk very fast! The assistant walked directly to me and said "Mr Hitchcock feels that it disturbs him that you're watching him. Would you please leave the set?" And I was kicked out ... after *Jaws*! And I never met him!' Spielberg's biographer Tony Crawley pointed out that the Richard Dreyfuss characters in *Jaws* (1975) and *Close Encounters of the Third Kind* (1977) are screen descendants of the 'common man' as portrayed by Cary Grant in *North by Northwest*. It was as much Truffaut's book on Hitchcock as his acting abilities that made Spielberg cast François Truffaut as the scientist in *Close Encounters*. (Despite the language barrier, the director and his star communicated musically, whistling their favorite Bernard Herrmann themes from Hitchcock films to each other between shots.)

Family Plot is a rich, assured film, as one would expect from such a venerable director as Hitchcock, but it is also a surprisingly buoyant and exuberant film, the work of a young enthusiast, not an accomplished master. William Devane is a memorable addition to the glowing list of Hitchcock villains, his Anderson echoing the 'ordinariness' of James Mason's Vandamm and Claude Rains' Alexander Sebastian. As Hitchcock explained to John Russell Taylor while filming *Family Plot*: 'People always think villains are extraordinary, but in my experience they are usually rather ordinary and boring ... In this story, the way I see it, the villains are actually rather dull characters, they are the straight men if you like, their motives are very ordinary and mundane. Whereas the more ordinary couple are actually very peculiar ... It makes it less melodramatic, lighter and more believable ...' Barbara Harris and Bruce Dern are suitably baffled and bewildered as the hapless heroine and hero, and the film has more cinematic legerdemain than we have any right to expect from a director in his sixth decade of filmmaking. The most bizarre and spectacular of Adamson and Fran's kidnappings is that of a bishop in mid-service, a set piece which Hitchcock told John Russell Taylor he relished: 'Kidnap him in ordinary clothes alone in a wood and he might as well be a stockbroker. If you're going to kidnap a Bishop, you want to do it at the moment when he is most evidently being a Bishop – in the middle of Mass in front of a crowded congregation!'

Central to the film, and what fascinated Hitchcock most, is the element of chance in everyday life. We follow George and Blanche until Fran happens to walk in front of their car at traffic lights, and suddenly we are off and running on a totally different thread. The destinies of two couples in San Francisco are now inextricably linked. It is a return to the random selection of *Rear Window* when, with all the apartments to choose from, James Stewart is drawn to Raymond Burr's. But out of the 'eight million stories in the naked city' here we focus on two sets of characters whose lives unexpectedly cross.

Ernest Lehman showed that in the years which had elapsed between *North by Northwest* and *Family Plot* he had lost none of his sleight of hand, and in tandem with Hitchcock produced the old magic even without Cary Grant. The similarity between the two films extended even to having a runaway car sequence in both. In *North by Northwest* Grant was hopelessly drunk; in *Family Plot* George's (Bruce Dern's) car has been tampered with and goes out of control on a steep mountain road. The sequence builds and builds as Blanche (Barbara Harris) thinks he is just driving recklessly to scare her! It is a perfectly shot sequence, alternating between high comedy and high adventure. There is also a beautifully balanced sequence in a cemetery (the family plot of the title) where the characters progress along the neatly laid out patchwork of paths, like characters in a human chess game. This scene prompted much earnest analysis of the 'symbolism,' but Ernest Lehman recalled debunking a French journalist's thesis about the car numberplate: 'I hate to tell you but the reason I used that licence plate number was that it used to be my own and I felt it would be legally safe to use!' Perhaps it is also 'symbolic' that in what was to be his very last cameo appearance, the familiar outline of Hitchcock's figure is seen in the office of the Registrar of Births and Deaths. It was a fitting farewell.

After the disappointments of *Torn Curtain* and *Topaz* and the patchiness of *Frenzy*, *Family Plot* was a totally appropriate swansong. Early in the film Julia tells Blanche 'I'm 78 years of age and I'd like to go to my grave with a quiet conscience.' Hitchcock was 77 when he shot that scene. Of course, it was not known then that Hitch's 53rd film was to be his last – he retained his desire to work to the very end of his life. But critics delightedly recognized it as a masterly film from an old master. *Sight & Sound* called it 'a marvellously fluid light comedy with scarcely a slack moment, it blithely omits murder entirely ... *Family Plot* can be seen as a veritable testament – a measured assessment by the director of his methods that, by evaluating what is and isn't essential to them, clarifies everything in his career preceding it.' *The Illustrated London News* found it 'full of benign mischief, beautiful craftsmanship and that elusive sense of cinematic rhythm that has always been Hitchcock's trump card.'

Hitchcock's real trump card, though, was his unfailing ability to shock and entertain. He never allowed himself to rest on his laurels. For over half a century, Alfred Hitchcock had achieved unparallelled acclaim and devotion in the fickle world of cinema. *Family Plot* completed a body of work which is unlikely ever to be equalled in cinema. Hitchcock acolyte Steven Spielberg will have to keep going at the same prodigious pace until 2021 before he can equal Hitchcock's output. The cinema has changed again since *Family Plot* (*Close Encounters* and *Star Wars* opened the following year) and a survey in 1985 revealed that a quarter of all cinema tickets sold in the USA were for either a Steven Spielberg or a Sylvester Stallone film. But Hitchcock's career still encompasses the very beginning of cinema and its current technological excesses. There is not, frankly, anyone like him around now – George Cukor and Orson Welles are dead and only John Huston, Billy Wilder and David Lean have the pedigree and durability to be in Hitchcock's league.

Below: *Twenty years on and things still haven't changed at the Bates Motel – Anthony Perkins in* Psycho II *(1983).*

Hitchcock's health had been failing and in 1972 he had a pacemaker inserted – which he delighted in showing off to visiting journalists. Close friends were worried about his health and failing memory. Alma had recovered well from her stroke, but the two were now grandparents, and old age was taking its toll, with Hitchcock suffering badly from arthritis. He had few interests beside the cinema and what he needed now was a film to occupy him. So, becoming increasingly interested in *The Short Night*, about British spy George Blake, Hitchcock began work with screenwriter David Newman on a screenplay. Speaking to John Russell Taylor about *The Short Night* in 1977, Hitchcock described in some detail the breathtaking opening scene he had all mapped out. It was to be set outside Wormwood Scrubs prison, with Blake's accomplice talking to the spy via a walkie-talkie hidden in a bunch of flowers, helping Blake to escape during the weekly prison film show.

In 1977 Hitchcock stressed again that he was not ready for retirement, even at 78, and pointed to his contract with Universal which required two further films after *Family Plot*. When John Russell Taylor asked if he ever feared the competition from his past Hitchcock's answer was revealing: 'Inevitably, sometimes. But probably less the longer you're at it. Look at that young man Spielberg, making the biggest moneymaker ever so early in his career. How was he going to top that? I find the thing to do is to concentrate entirely on the film in hand; and say to yourself, it's only a movie!' This sentiment echoes down the years, from the teenage Alfred making his way through the streets of the East End, avidly devouring the latest American silent films, through his

caption work, his tentative experiments with sound, his classic evocation of Britain and the British character, his exile in America, his journeys into the darker psyche of the human mind, through the optimism of the human spirit, through praise and damnation, wryly offering this advice to the actors and ultimately to us all: 'It's only a movie!'

This irreverence runs like a silver thread through Hitchcock's films and is nowhere more apparent than in the final shot of his last film. Barbara Harris looks straight into the camera and gives us a conspiratorial wink. Right to the end what singled Hitchcock out was the tremendous sense of fun he brought to even the most somber subject. In life this sense of humor manifested itself in his well-known penchant for practical jokes. On one occasion he wrote a bogus fan letter to Robert Donat: 'Dear Mr Doughnut, I think you are marvellous. When you come on I have passion. Please send me a photograph of yourself in short trousers.' He did receive a photograph, signed 'Robert Doughnut,' although unfortunately not in short trousers. Hitchcock went to all sorts of lengths to achieve the desired effect. On one occasion he employed an actress to play the part of a dinner guest, who he then proceeded to insult outrageously, much to the embarrassment of the real guests. Another time he smuggled a full size horse into an actor's dressing room.

Even after *Family Plot* and in his late seventies, Hitchcock resolutely denied any plans for retirement, but the films had stopped coming and it was widely assumed that his work was complete. In 1979 Ephraim Katz wrote: 'Hitchcock's art reached its full maturity with such superior thrillers as *Rear Window, Vertigo, North by Northwest* and *Psycho*. These films culminated one of the most illustrious directorial careers in the history of the cinema.'

The final honor came a few months before his death, when he became Sir Alfred Hitchcock. On 3 January 1980 a bizarre ceremony took place on a sound stage at Universal Studios when the British Consul General knighted the man who had been an American citizen for 25 years. It was to be his last public appearance before death came to him quietly on the morning of 29 April 1980.

Hitchcock's funeral took place in Hollywood and was attended by, among others, Tippi Hedren, Janet Leigh, Karl Malden, Anne Bancroft, Louis Jourdan, Eva Marie Saint and Mrs Gloria Stewart (representing her husband, James). In the funeral address Father Tom Sullivan said: 'He told me that the Jesuits scared the dickens out of him, so he thought he would make it his career to scare the dickens out of the world!'

In June 1980 a memorial service was held at Westminster Cathedral, London, where 40 years before Edmund Gwenn had plunged to his death in *Foreign Correspondent*. Sir John Mills read the lesson and in attendance were Ingrid Bergman, Lord and Lady Bernstein, Ann Todd and Barry Foster. The BBC paid tribute the following night by screening *Blackmail* with which, over half a century before, Hitchcock had introduced sound to the British cinema.

His beloved Alma survived him by only two years, and on her death the Hitchcock estate (estimated to be in the region of £20 million) went in its entirety to their only daughter Patricia.

While still alive Hitchcock collaborated extensively with Francois Truffaut, whose book *Hitchcock* was the most re-

Opposite: *Norman Bates in* Psycho II.

vealing insight into the Master's craft when published in 1968. In 1976 Donald Spoto's superb analytic study of Hitchcock's films was published, *The Art of Alfred Hitchcock*. This featured an introduction by Princess Grace of Monaco and was enthusiastically received by Hitchcock himself. The 'authorized biography,' written in conjunction with the Hitchcock family, came out in 1978. John Russell Taylor offered a less penetrating analysis of the films, but gave a much needed insight into Hitchcock's life.

The most controversial book on Hitchcock was not published until three years after his death, when Donald Spoto returned to Hitchcock's life and career and produced an exhaustive portrait of a complex man in *The Life of Alfred Hitchcock: The Dark Side of Genius* (1983). Hitchcock's daughter Patricia was happy with John Russell Taylor's authorized biography and did not wish to co-operate on another book. So Spoto worked on his subject from the outside, detailing many of Hitchcock's obsessions, fantasies and neuroses. He produced an iconoclastic work which burrowed to the heart of Hitchcock's psyche and the way in which it manifested itself in his films. The image which came across was of a man haunted by his past, largely misogynist and with a streak of cruelty that at times ran into sadism. Spoto's thesis was that Hitchcock's 'delight in his craft could never be liberated from a terrifying heritage of desire and concomitant guilt.' The book caused a terrific furore, particularly as it came in the wake of similarly controversial biographies of other such cinematic venerables as Joan Crawford, Peter Sellers and Bing Crosby. Spoto's book was serialized in the *Daily Mail* under the gloating headline 'Haunted By Sexual Fantasies ... He Turned Stars Into Slaves.' In his review of the book, John Russell Taylor acutely commented: 'One starts to wonder why, if Hitchcock was such a monster, so many of his professional associates stayed with him for so long!' The general view was summed up by Philip French in *The Observer*: 'The book in no way diminishes Hitchcock's stature as one of the authentic geniuses of the popular cinema, and it left me with a greater understanding of, if less affection for, the Old Master.' Colleagues of Hitchcock who still retained a great deal of affection for him leapt swiftly to his defense. Ivor Montagu, who worked closely with him in the 1920s, said: 'Was he a kind man? I should say so: certainly, also a family man. Was he cruel? No. When I knew him, and doubtless later, he loved practical jokes, but I never knew him play one except as part of a tit for tat series with a friend.' James Stewart reacted to the book thus: 'A dark side, as ascribed in the biography, has to come out all the time. A man can't hide it from the people he wants to hide it from, from the people who are close to him. I got to know him pretty well, and I don't believe there *was* a dark side.'

'The Final Hitchcock Mystery,' as it became known, concerned the fate of five of his key films which for years had been unavailable for viewing. Despite efforts by film theaters and television companies, *Rope, Rear Window, The Trouble with Harry, Vertigo* and the remake of *The Man Who Knew Too Much* could not be seen anywhere. *Rear Window* was out of circulation due to a dispute with the estate of the author and the rights to the remaining four films had reverted from Universal to Hitchcock and at one stage Hitchcock was keen to destroy the films. However, wisdom prevailed and they remained locked away and unseen. Leslie Halliwell, one of the UK's leading television buyers, recalled dealing with Hitchcock's agent Herman Citron: 'We had been trying to get these pictures for years, we would get through to Citron and he would ask "How much?" When we told him, it was never enough.' The situation was resolved happily with the rerelease of the five films in 1983; the familiar portly profile of the director appeared on posters proclaiming them 'The Essential Hitchcock.'

If imitation is the sincerest form of flattery, then Alfred Hitchcock could not be more flattered. Aside from the young French directors of the 'new wave' in the 1950s, Hitchcock's most public imitator is the director Brian de Palma. A film-maker of some promise (his *Phantom of the Paradise* [1974] and *Blow Out* [1981] were indications of a real talent at work), de Palma has unfortunately let his Hitchcock obsession get the better of him. This manifested itself with *Obsession* (1976) where he even went to the extent of using Hitchcock's erstwhile composer Bernard Herrmann. *Obsession* is uncomfortably close to *Vertigo*, with a sprinkling of Nicolas Roeg's *Don't Look Now* (1973) thrown in for good measure. Cliff Robertson is obsessed by the memory of his wife who was kidnapped and died in a rescue attempt. Years later in Venice he spots Genevieve Bujold, who is the spitting image of his late wife. Hitchcock references pepper the film – the villain is murdered with a pair of scissors recalling *Dial M For Murder*, the locked room at the top of the house brings back memories of *Rebecca* and the shadow of *Vertigo* is never more than a frame away. De Palma's *Dressed to Kill* (1980) apes *Psycho*, and comes complete with shower scenes at the beginning *and* end; while his *Body Double* (1985) pillaged *Vertigo* again, with

Craig Wesson's claustrophobia rendering him unable to prevent a murder – just like James Stewart's acrophobia 27 years before. The core of the film is drawn from *Rear Window*, with Wesson observing the erotic goings-on in an apartment across the valley, but the voyeurism is far more explicit than in the Hitchcock film and gradually degenerates into limp pornography.

Claude Chabrol, co-author with Eric Rohmer of one of the first authoritative critical studies of Hitchcock in 1957, and a filmmaker of distinction, notably for his Hitchcock-inspired *Le Boucher* (1967), commented in 1985: 'I think his (Hitchcock's) influence on de Palma is completely external. Not that it's less interesting, just that de Palma tries to capture the sort of gut sensations he's felt at the time of making the film. The trouble is, on the level of pure, immediate sensation, the film starts off pastiching Hitchcock, then in the middle he thinks "okay, that's enough of that." That's what I felt about *Body Double* – the first half is almost an exact copy of *Rear Window* and *Vertigo* rolled together, then he's had enough of that and goes into the porn story, which is quite amusing, but not as good as the first part.'

Director John Frankenheimer, renowned for *The Birdman of Alcatraz* (1961) and *The Manchurian Candidate* (1962), speaking of Hitchcock said: 'Any American director who says he hasn't been influenced by him is out of his mind!' Hitchcock's influence does indeed seem inescapable and can be discerned in films as diverse as John Boulting's *Brighton Rock* (1943), Antonioni's *The Passenger* (1975), Coppola's *The Conversation* (1974), Arthur Penn's *Night Moves* (1975), Sidney Lumet's *Deathtrap* (1982) and right up to the present with Peter Weir's acclaimed *Witness* (1985), with Harrison Ford seeking sanctuary with the Amish.

Below: *Brian de Palma's* Obsession *(1976) was a virtual remake of* Vertigo, *with Cliff Robertson and Genevieve Bujold.*
Opposite: *Hitchcock on location in the 1960s.*

The ultimate tribute came with Mel Brooks' loving homage to the *spirit* of Hitchcock's work, *High Anxiety* (1977). The film began with the unequivocal credit 'This film is dedicated to the Master of Suspense Alfred Hitchcock.' Drawing amusingly on *Spellbound*, the film was set at an 'Institute For The Very, Very Nervous.' Other in-jokes included references to *Vertigo, Psycho, Rope, North by Northwest* and *The Birds*. But perhaps the nicest touch is when a hotel reservation is altered by a 'Mr MacGuffin!'

Like the great artist he was, much as he denied it, Hitchcock's art and influence live on after his death. The latest homage, in a long line which shows no sign of abating, came in January 1986 when the BBC screened *The MacGuffin*, a film about a film critic obsessed with Hitchcock, and living out *Rear Window* in Notting Hill. Another tribute came in British Film Year in 1985 when Hitchcock was one of only five of cinema's greatest artists chosen to appear on a set of commemorative stamps.

In the definitive *International Film Encyclopedia*, Ephraim Katz encapsulated Hitchcock's continuing appeal to audiences: 'They continue to flock to every Hitchcock film on the strength of the director's name alone, expecting and getting exhilarating entertainment from the grandest wizard of cinema magic the screen has ever known.' This is Hitchcock's triumph: that his genius survives him – a body of work which must stand forever unequalled.

Above: *Claude Chabrol's Hitchcock-style* Le Boucher *(1967).*
Below: *The portrait used for the British Film Year stamps.*
Opposite: *Seen here in the studio in the 1940s, the last of the cinema greats – Alfred Hitchcock.*

Index

Page numbers in italics refer to illustrations

BIBLIOGRAPHY

Agee, James *On Film* Peter Owen, 1963
Barrow, Kenneth *Mr Chips: The Life of Robert Donat* Methuen, 1985
Butler, Ivan *The Making of Feature Films – A Guide* Pelican, 1971
Crawley, Tony *The Steven Spielberg Story* Zomba, 1983
Englund, Steven *Princess Grace* Sphere, 1985
Eyles, Allen *James Stewart* W H Allen, 1984
Goldman, William *Adventures in the Screen Trade* Futura, 1985
Greene, Graham *The Pleasure Dome* Secker & Warberg, 1972
Halliwell, Leslie *Filmgoers Companion, Eighth Edition* Granada, 1984
Halliwell, Leslie *Film Guide, 5th Edition* Granada, 1985
Higham, Charles *Charles Laughton: An Intimate Biography* W H Allen, 1976
Katz, Ephraim *The International Film Encyclopedia* Papermac, 1982
Mason, James *Before I Forget* Hamish Hamilton, 1981
Morley, Sheridan *Tales from the Hollywood Raj* Coronet, 1985
Orwell, George *Decline of the English Murder* Penguin, 1965
Russell Taylor, John *Hitch* Abacus, 1981
Selznick, David O *Memo From . . .* (selected and edited by Rudy Behlmer) Macmillan, 1972
Spoto, Donald *The Art of Alfred Hitchcock* Dolphin, 1979
Spoto, Donald *The Life of Alfred Hitchcock: The Dark Side of Genius* Collins, 1983
Steinberg, Cobbett *Reel Facts* Penguin, 1981
Truffaut, François *Hitchcock* Panther, 1969
Walker, Alexander *Double Takes* Elm Tree, 1977
Wright, Basil *The Long View: An International History of Cinema* Paladin, 1976

Acknowledgments

The publisher would like to thank Jane Laslett the editor, Richard Garratt the designer, Jean Martin the picture researcher and Ron Watson who compiled the index. Our thanks to the film distribution companies, and special thanks to the National Film Archive, London who supplied all of the illustrations except for the following:

Academy of Motion Picture Arts and Sciences: page 16(bottom), 59, 70(top), 82(bottom), 149(top), 177(bottom left)
BBC Hulton Picture Library: page 172(top)
The Billy Rose Theatre Collection, The New York Public Library at Lincoln Center: pages 149(bottom), 180(main illustration)
Bison Picture Library: pages 108(bottom), 122(top), 126(bottom left), 143(top).
Bundesarchiv: page 87(top)
CIC Video: pages 132(top), 137, 154(top right), 174, 183
Jerry Ohlinger's: pages 12(top), 33(top left), 72, 84, 133, 134(both), 161, 170, 172(bottom), 173(bottom), 176, 184, 187
Manny Warman, Columbia University: page 178
Museum of Modern Art, New York: pages 32(bottom), 34(top), 55, 64, 65, 69, 73, 80, 92, 102, 108(top right), 119, 148(both), 189
National Portrait Gallery, London: page 188(bottom)
The Rank Organization plc: pages 41, 43, 45(top), 49(bottom left), 57(top)
TPS/Central Press: pages 173(top), 182(top)
TPS/Fox: page 35(bottom)
TPS/Keystone: pages 60(bottom), 82(top), 103(top left), 130(top right), 156(top)